If I was Jesus…

Matt Chapman & JR Baker

Introduction

In Ephesians Paul tells me to imitate God. Most of this book has come from that challenge.

The premise for this book is simple. It's also – possibly - incredibly blasphemous. The idea came to me while I was lying in the sun, exhausted after having been asked to smash up an old aviary in our back garden by my wife.

I hate doing garden work. I hate it only slightly less than I hate vacuuming and only slightly more than doing the washing up. The only saving grace about this particular task had been that it had allowed me to purchase a new sledgehammer. I chose to name it Sledric. For most of that particular day Sledric and I had knocked this old aviary to kingdom-come and afterwards there I lay, utterly exhausted.

Earlier, as the afternoon had worn on and as I had beaten the stubborn wooden timbers (each rotten with age and sodden with years of soaked-in bird muck which somehow endowed it with superhuman resistance to my blows), I'd started thinking;

Life's not bad. I just turned 30. For my birthday I went mountain biking in the Lake District with 8 other guys resulting in a tremendous crash, scraped helmet and buckled wheel. Then my pregnant wife and 3 dogs joined us at the cabin we'd rented and we just hung out for a week in the snow. That was how I celebrated my 30th birthday.

Pausing Sledrics swings I'd lent on his handle and it suddenly hit me;

Jesus celebrated turning 30 by announcing to the world he was the son of God…

…I got a bottle of whiskey from my friends and a parachute jump from my wife…

…Jesus went out to the desert, started his ministry and ultimately got himself killed just a few years later.

Standing there in my Spiderman t-shirt (a source of constant marital consternation) and leaning on a sledgehammer I'd nicknamed, I suddenly realized that I was now Jesus' age. For as long as I'd remembered I'd always pictured Jesus as being much older and wiser. Much more Moses-like. Beardier. Weathered. Tainted with experience. Certainly much more different than me. But now the older-bit isn't true. Jesus was my age at the start of the gospels and suddenly the call for imitation had become a much closer prospect than before.

All of this was mulling around in my head over the next hour as I got back up, became sweatier and sweatier, angrier and angrier at the stone foundations (that I surmised must have originally been forged to hide the Ark of the Covenant they were so solid and reinforced) and finally all came together into a stream of awkward thoughts;

I bet Jesus never had to do this.

I bet Jesus never flinched when a spider (albeit one the size of a wombat) scuttled out from behind a floorboard. I bet Jesus never hit his wrist with a hammer and tried not to swear or accidentally rubbed Macaw Parrot droppings over his face. In fact I bet Jesus never had to sweat like this, never had to work like this...

Finally, finished for the day and lying back on the grass, surveying my destruction all these thoughts finally came together.

If Jesus had needed an aviary demolished could He could have just looked skyward and winked. Would the wood have simply flat-packed itself into easily removable piles and some nearby forest animals scurry up to take it away for their nests, leaving his work easily complete?

I started wondering about how Jesus made his trade in carpentry. How did He price up His goods and sort out making a profit? What were his margins? Did he occasionally pray that the chest of drawers He was working on would turn out fine?

Did he ever stay up late working overtime on a particular table that needed to be made in time for the local dignitary? Did he sweat over tasks or, as God, could He always count on Himself to finish in-time and on-budget? Did he ever think he was better at woodwork than he actually was, bite off more than he could chew and fail to properly finish the underside of a table, leaving it unfinished and awkwardly leaning against a garage wall for an

4

entire year (an autobiographical comment, but still valid, I felt)?

Was he ever forced to throw some of his handiwork in the dump when someone begged him to "finally move that monstrosity I'd made"? Again, autobiographical but valid.

But seriously, I wondered, did He ever do a rubbish job of making shelves? Did anyone ever complain?

If he was my age when he was wrapping up his carpentry career I began picturing myself in his place. I began wondering what I'd do if I'd been in Jesus' position. I tried to imagine the stink of the streets and the hot middle-eastern sun, pounding down on the stacks of wood waiting to be sawn.

I started wondering about tea breaks (well…I am a fireman and it is a job priority) and about the job satisfaction you'd get from working all day with basic tools. Of leaning on the doorframe of the workshop after a hard day and taking a cool drink. Of feeling proud of whatever carpentry achievements I'd made.

And that's how I started wondering about what I would do *If I was Jesus*.

I thought about how, *If I was Jesus*, I don't think I'd have been able to settle for Nazareth. I'd use my power to become the greatest carpenter, the greatest woodsman, the greatest *artist* that that little town had ever produced. I'd have moved onwards and upwards.

Lying on my garden in Leeds, watching the sun go down it suddenly hit me; *If I was Jesus* would I have been happy to be a carpenter for 20 or so years? Jesus could quite easily have been a world-famous artist, a philosopher, a leader, a King even as well as being the son of God. Anything other than just a bog-standard carpenter.

Even if He did stay as a woodworker He could have made the wood grow itself into the most expensive, finest, most desirable dining room sets this side of Ikea and still had time to die for humanities sins. Eternal salvation on offer as well as a first-rate, world-class coffee table - now that'd be a savior I could more imagine myself being.

And here lies the root of my questioning; if I'm honest I have always, secretly wanted to be a superhero.

The point of the matter is that unfortunately, no matter how hard I try to fly, no matter how much I try and levitate coffee cups or wear my pants outside my trousers and try and fight crime I simply don't have what it takes to be a superhero.

But Jesus did.

If I was Jesus, I started reasoning that I could have done incredible things. Perhaps not crime fighting (capes were never in-vogue in Palestine), but I could certainly have made more of the incredible gifts and abilities He had. *If I was Jesus,* I wondered, what wouldn't I do? How could I have dealt with the Roman occupation? What would I have done with the Pharisees? What would I have done with His ability to read minds? *How different would the gospels have turned out, had I been Jesus?*

At first I simply imagined that there would simply be less "hanging out with lepers" and more "turning the Pharisees into kittens", but despite the jokey premise I couldn't get the thought out of my mind.

Later on that week I spoke to my best mate JR Baker about what I'd been thinking and about an idea to put some stuff down on paper. Seeing as he is actually vastly less holy and spiritual than me he said not to worry about the potential blasphemy.

And thus, this book came about. It's his fault.

And so the idea for this book is simple. I, Matt Chapman, am a normal human being. I think I'm a pretty good specimen of an average guy. I'm not an academic theologian and let's face it, if you're reading this book and not "Professor Gragglesteins 96 volume thesis on the doctrine of hereditary baldness and the essential, if hidden, part it plays in the construction of the Pentateuch", you're probably not one either.

The point of this book isn't to see what a theologically trained professor would do differently, *if they were Jesus*. It's to see what a normal man would do.

And as far as that premise goes JR and I have made up some

simple rules;

Rule 1.

The perspective is from a 'good' man

We're not writing this to see what would have happened if Hitler was Jesus. We're not writing this to see what would have happened if an evil man had been Jesus or even a good atheist. We're writing this to see what would have happened if I - a reasonably decent if flawed, Christian guy was Jesus. How His life and experiences would have differed if I'd been Him.

Despite not being Hitler however, I am a massive sinner. I am not the perfect lamb of God. I am going to write this (sometimes by playing devil's advocate) from a flawed man's perspective.

Rule 2.

JR writes the real story

This isn't just a fiction book. We wanted to put some interesting ideas across about how Jesus' life would have altered if I'd been Him, but we also want to look at why Jesus did it the way He did as well.

I'm going to write the fictional stories about *If I was Jesus* and then I'm going to email them to JR. As a trained minister (and not merely a firefighter trained in…fighting fire) he'll receive them (whilst no doubt deep in holy thought inside a monastery somewhere or as he goes about healing the sick or whatever it is that he does) and then he'll reply. I'll then try and translate them from Texan into English and then write the next bit, and on and on.

Rule 3.

I have to actually tell you who JR Baker is

Ok, JR doesn't actually live in a monastery. He doesn't have a rainbow-strapped acoustic guitar and he doesn't (to my knowledge) bash anyone with bibles. He is, however, quite simply the single best human being I know. He's not a clichéd Christian; he's a basketball playing, goofy, hilarious American minister who I've had the great pleasure of knowing for 12 years now. I was honored to be the best man at his wedding, and he's the godfather of my little boy Noah.

We don't always agree on everything (the finale of Lost was soul-crushingly bad and despite what he says he secretly knows it. The end, no more arguments) but one thing I know as an absolute truth – this man knows God. He knows his theology and if anyone can actually sort through my rubbish thoughts and find something worthwhile within, it's him. He's my best mate and the only person I'd turn to (I <u>have</u> turned to) in a crisis of faith.

Rule 4.

We won't worry about offending

None of this is meant to be blasphemous. I don't think I'm Jesus. I don't think I'll ever be Jesus. That's not the point.

This book isn't supposed to annoy anyone. It's supposed to be a chance for us to think about why Jesus lived the way He did and how remarkable that was. Obviously I'm going to write some things that are going to sound bad to some people when I describe what would happen *If I was Jesus*.

Please don't be offended. God gave us freedom, grace and forgiveness so I don't think he's going to take offence at what I have to say. He was the one who gave us nostril hair, the aardvark and Finland and therefore I can confidently state that He has a sense of humor.

Rule 5

I will eventually stop pre-ambling and just get on with it.

Enough said.

Here we go then. Eight chapters describing what would have happened in eight events throughout the gospels, *If I was Jesus*.

Chapter One

John's Baptism

Everyone right now, over every corner of Galilee is talking about me. Amazing!

I'm more popular than open-toed-sandals and more of a controversy than Zechariah-the-Dullards latest psalm release (*"Methuselah's Birthdays"* - 969 verses recounting in depth each and every present he received).

Basically I'm a star.

I'm the biggest thing since the invention of the straight road. I'm hotter than a fattened calf at Rosh HaShannah. I'm like a lamp lit at Sukkot - I'm burning up. I'm as fresh as - well, you get the idea.

And do you know what? For the first time I feel like the real me. I'm finally doing what I'm supposed to do. No more sawdust behind my fingernails. No more blisters from holding a hammer all day. Finally I'm not sitting around anymore or skulking in the shadows, waiting for my time to come. I'm out there doing it. Off the leash earlier than expected (it'll be even more of a shock to the old fuddy-duddy's when a young guy like me starts schooling them!) and ready to bring the Kingdom of Heaven near.

The baptism was amazing. I couldn't have hoped that It'd have gone any better. I was so excited this morning that I literally sprinted down to the Jordan. John was already there and the crowds were heaving to hear him. I let him finish his speech (he was tearing into the Pharisees again; I got butterflies when I saw that they were there too. Finally a chance to rub it in their faces after having to sit through so many boring sermons over the years) only nearly stepping in when I heard him call them "White Washed tombs".

I'm all for "shock and awe" but there's definitely a time and a place. I don't want people to be put off my message by coming on too strong and I certainly don't want anyone feeling sorry for the Pharisees either. In the end though I figured that John's harshness might actually work in my favor. It might make me look even more tolerant, even more gracious, so I let him continue.

Finally, as he started his baptisms I knew it was time for me to take center stage. Pushing past a few of the elderly men who were struggling down to the water-line I looked over the edge, took a run up and jumped straight in.

Now before you question my motives, please remember this; I (obviously) never got to see the whole "star above" that guided the shepherds and wise men to where I was born. That whole story has galled me since first hearing about it as a child. A manger?! Me?!!

No wonder no one knew who I was, growing up! I'll never understand the motivation for doing it that way and I can only guess that it was some kind of angelic clerical error that sent me to Bethlehem and not Rome or Jerusalem. I'll never understand why it's been made so hard for people to believe I'm the King.

I can just about remember the temple-incident from when I was a boy (mainly just my dad's worried face and the feeling that I was probably grounded when we got back home) but even that didn't materialize into the miraculous beginning I'd hoped for. So this, for me, was it.

This was the moment I'd been waiting for my whole life. The big explosion I'd been day-dreaming about for years. This was to be my pay-off for every single night of uncomfortable sleep I'd had to put up with on that wooden bench. The moment that God told everyone the mystery I'd been hiding, the moment my secret identity was revealed, the moment the worlds hero was unveiled. I figured that if I'm going to die for these people the least I can get is a good introduction, eh?!

When I'd lie in bed all those nights and imagined the moment that people found out that I was the Messiah I'd pictured the earth cracking open. Flocks of doves filling the sky and chorus-lines of angels bombarding the terrified crowds with trumpet blasts.

As it transpired however, at first it seemed as if I was heading for a crushing disappointment. Picture the scene; I'm at the Jordan. I run. I jump. I wait. I'd hit the water and thrown out my arms, closed my eyes, head thrust heavenward. I'd smiled and waited for the inevitable angelic music to begin.

After a few moments I did think that I could sort-of see a bit of a light behind my shut eyes, and perhaps hear a slight whisper from somewhere, but my ears were listening for mighty cherubim and seraphim not odd whispers.

After more moments of awkward silence I opened one eye and peered out. Instead of all-powerful beings singing my praises all I could see were confused gawps from the crowd and hear angry mutters. They were all assuming I'd tried to jump the queue. Only when one of the kids from the crowd pulled away from his mother and kicked a shower of dirty water at me did the mood soften and the laughter began.

Spitting out what little had got into my mouth, pulling a small bit of twig from my lip; I ignored the sweet little child and closed my eyes again. I guessed there must simply have been a delay in Michael getting there on-time. That was when the child ran into the water himself and gave me a dead-leg.

I imagine that there is little in life more un-Messiah-like than the sight of a grown man yelping in pain and hobbling forwards, slipping on a flat rock underwater and floundering into a lake. The only saving grace was that after I finally found my way to my feet I knew I had absolutely everyone's attention.

After the temptation to turn the brat into a bird had faded I tried to brush myself down, spat out the wad of reeds I'd swallowed and waded out to John. Seeing me he turned and smiled, sweeping my shoulders clear of what mud remained. His hand suddenly paused and I saw something in his face; a kind of recognition and awe that I hadn't ever seen before.

Now you see the thing with John is that no matter how famous he's gotten I still see the 8 year old boy who'd convinced me it was Abrahamic law to pee on your sandals to clean off the "evil mud" on the Sabbath. The hiding I received from dad about that has pretty much solidified my cousins image as the naughty runt laughing at his naïve cousin, rather than the renowned prophet he'd since become. But at that moment John the man, the prophet, spoke. His voice cracking slightly he muttered;

"Why do you come to me? I…I need to be baptized by you.."

I had been working on my smile for occasions such as these; head tilted slightly, eyes half closed, no teeth, no grin, just a gentle raise of the lip. Something that says "ah, sweet sinner, I understand your pain/problem/lack of wisdom and can empathize with you (even though obviously I'm far, far superior and beyond your wildest imagination)". It was this smile that I now gave John, putting my hand on his shoulder before answering softly back;

"Yes John. Yes indeed you do."

He opened his eyes and looked as if he wanted to speak again before I stuck my knee into his and quickly dunked him under the water. Pulling him out I patted his back hard, helping to clear the water he'd swallowed and pushed him off towards the crowd. John had been a great warm up act but now it was time for the crowd to see the main event.

They were all still looking at me and I knew what they were thinking (seriously, I knew it, I could hear it. Most of it is unrepeatable here...) and knew it was time to make my mark. Two thoughts were most common in the crowd at that moment; "Why on earth is the woodworker here?" and "If he's going to make a speech, has he brought biscuits along? I'd really like some biscuits."

Now at this point I was kind of winging it. I'd been thrown by the lack of pizazz. I'd expected at the very least a thunderclap. But there'd been no sign from heaven, no angelic musical interlude. Some of the crowd started to peel away, frustrated. I needed a miracle and I needed one fast.

"What do people like?" I asked myself, "what will keep these people interested? What can I offer them, that will stop them from missing out on Gods amazing offer He was about to present to them?" Then it hit me; two words. Free booze.

"Does anyone have a cup with them?" I asked, my voice faltering slightly at first before I coughed it clear "Anyone? Just a standard cup?"

Finally (out of pity at me publicly humiliating myself, I think), a lady took a small bowl out of her sons pack and reluctantly tossed it over from the bank to me.

Frowning, concentrating, I swept my hand over the top of it with what I imagined to be a look of mystery, suspense and intrigue on my face. In hindsight this would have worked better had the kid from earlier not laughed out loud. Certainly his giggles stole some of the moment's gravitas and I had to really wrestle with the urge to turn his arms into cauliflowers. I did manage to ignore him though and finally spoke in hushed whispers;

"Watch now...watch, people...look, there's nothing inside the bowl, is there?" I waved it slowly around the crowd and even let

14

one child hold it, turning it over in his hand. I pulled my sleeves up, showing them again that there was nothing in them.

Taking it back I bent down, scooping up some of the river water into it. Again I slowly took it around the crowd and showed them the clear liquid, even dipping my finger in it and tasting it before them (as grim as that sounds I had already swallowed enough of the river at that point that I barely tasted anything).

Finally, placing it on my upturned hand, I stretched it out towards them. Holding my other hand over the bowl I fluttered my fingers and shut my eyes, mumbling noises under my breath.

Holding on to the pause for much longer than I needed to I finally let my body slump with what I hoped looked like a release of energy. Knowing it had changed I nonchalantly wandered back to the now-curious crowd and calmly passed it back to the woman, smiling and winking at her son as I asked her to go ahead and drink it.

She did. And then she screamed. Bingo. The bowl was quickly passed around the crowd as I coolly walked back to the middle of the river, the roar of the crowd growing as more and more of them tasted the "Galilee vintage '31" full bodied red that I'd just made.

Finally, after I'd milked the excitement enough, I held my hands up for silence. This was it. This was my moment, my entrance. This had to be how Dad wanted me to start my ministry. He'd always been a fan of showmanship – Carmel, Mount Zion, The red sea – and now it was my time. Fair enough, birth me into a shed. But now was my time to shine.

The crowd were in the palm of my hand and I knew I could do one of 2 things. I could draw a great analogy about them being the water in the bowl and me being the catalyst that turned them into fine wine etc. I could use this opportunity to tell them about Gods kingdom, and about what they needed to do to be saved, yadda yadda yadda.

Or I could just bust out another miracle. I mean what if they'd missed the water/wine trick? The crowd on the other side of the river hadn't seen it so surely they deserved a sign too? It was a no-brainer really and I knew just what to do.

I had already spotted the man on crutches when I'd arrived and now I pointed silently, ominously to him. I beckoned him to step into the water. Slowly, awkwardly, aided by his friends he did so.

I walked over, tightening my gut and puffing my chest out. My eyes were firm, my jaw set as I strode confidently through the water (I did stumble once but carried it off as a quickly kneeled-prayer, glancing heavenwards and pointing as I found my footing) and made my way towards him. Coming face to face, I placed my hand firmly on his head, turned back to the crowd and hushed them once more.

"What's your name my son?"

He was looking up at my hand, seemingly a little irritated at the river water pouring down his head;

"Son? I'm 65 years old you cheeky…"

I squeezed the top of his head slightly, smiling at him and gritting my teeth,

"Tell them your name…"

"Daniel."

"Well Dan…can I call you Dan?"

"No, my name is…"

"Tell me Dan, how long have you been…?" I didn't know how to address the issue of his leg so I just mimicked an accentuated limp.

"In Galilee?"

"No Dan, how long have you been…you know?" I bobbed my head up and down trying to nod towards his leg.

"A…chicken?" came his confused answer.

I gave up. "How long have you been a cripple, Dan?"

He seemed a little offended but quickly launched into retelling the

16

story;

"Well it's an interesting tale actually. It all happened when I was in my 20's. What happened was that my sister was playing on the roof and I got up there to…"

"Thanks, Dan." I tried to continue;

"…try and help her out…it was two days before the Sabbath as I recall. No, three days. Wait, I tell a lie, it was two and it was one of those really hot days that just make you feel…"

"I said 'Thanks Dan'" I smilingly said through even more gritted teeth,

"…so anyways I had climbed up to help her because back then we…"

"Get behind me!" I said, squeezing his head and spinning him around in the lake to the other side of me. The crowd gasped as one.

Shutting my eyes I could hear him muttering something under his breath but ignored it. After a few seconds of dramatic pause I spoke again, as loudly and as confidently as I could;

"In that case Danny-boy…" I'd practiced this exact scenario every morning for a fortnight and performed like a professional, "Father God to your mercy we beg, come down here and fix Dannys wonky leg. In the name of the Father…in fact, in the name of MMMYYYY Father…"

I opened one eye, half-smiling and waited until the murmuring at this had stopped before lifting my free hand way above my head and raising my voice even further;

"DANNY, BE HEALED. SHAZAM!"

On reflection the 'SHAZAM' was probably unnecessary but it did bring a few more gasps from the younger members of the audience and to my delight the irritating child from earlier was so startled that he dropped his lunch into the lake. Opening my eyes and looking down the man was still squinting up at me with a mixture of suspicion and fear.

17

Giving him another one of my practiced smiles I spoke softly, dropping my arms in mock-exhaustion;

"How do you feel, Danny?"

"Well my head's wet"

At that, yes, I let frustration get the better of me and hoisted him up, booting his crutches away and shoving him back towards the crowd.

His first few steps were doddery (not aided by him slipping on the same rock I'd stumbled on) but then he started striding out. In an instant the crowd went wild. Daniel himself screamed as he grasped down at his now-strong legs, turning back towards me;

"What, what does it mean? How did you…who are you?" he began to ask.

And so here it was. This was it, this was my way in. My chance to tell them, my moment to kick start my ministry. The miracle had perfectly set me up to begin explaining to all of them about what God was planning.

The only slight hiccup was as I began my voice was instantly swamped by the cheers of the crowd. Within seconds Daniel himself was lost as more and more people swelled forwards, diving into the lake and charging towards me. Guessing that there would be plenty of time for chats about redemption and such later, I stepped up onto the other bank and yelled out;

"There's more of this, much, much more, so come and see my show next week in Galilee town center!! Bring a friend…lepers get in half price. All healings are as free as your eternal salvation!! And before I forget, I need to tell you that God wants you to…"

What happened next wasn't how I imagined my launch ceremony would end. I never got to finish my sentence, my voice trailing off as I suddenly became aware of the bodies throwing themselves closer and closer into the water. Getting up to me, their torsos wading frantically through the water I smiled and reached out, expecting warm embraces and loving hugs.

Instead scores of rough hands grabbed out towards me, their

owners desperate faces turning from amazement to desperation. Someone tore my tunic (the brown one I'd aired out especially for today) and I only managed to get free by slipping it off my back. It was swiftly swallowed up by the crowd, torn into sections, and a huge fist fight breaking out between the people who'd taken it.

Mothers began thrusting babies towards me and behind them I could see older women slipping into the river and getting pushed under by more rushing bodies.

In that moment I'm not ashamed to say that I made a run for it. Climbing up the bank more hands grabbed my ankles before I was able to tug free. I just managed to slip out of their grasp, sprinting off towards the town. Turning back, checking I was making headway against the following crowds, I could only see one figure that remained on the furthest bank.

John wasn't looking at me. He was looking down at his feet, his face downcast and concerned. Only as I turned the corner did I see him look upwards with a look of confusion. I didn't have time to ponder this though as I hurriedly turned corners hoping to lose the crowds in the smaller back streets.

And so that was it! Perhaps it wasn't the entrance I'd hoped for and maybe I did milk it a little at the end but I guess the point is that people are talking about me. My first main show is sold out with pre-bookings and it's only going to get bigger and bigger from then on in! There'll be plenty of time to talk at the smaller shows, but for now I'm banking on the fact that people want spectacle not speeches. They want a show not a lecture. They've had 300 years of silence; they need something special to startle them back into seeking salvation. I've certainly started that! By the time I make it to Jerusalem, Jesus-fever will be red-hot!
SHAZAM!

JR's Response

Well then here we are! I am supposed to be the one to give a super spiritual, holy response to all of that…wow!! Where do I even begin? First off, as has been said, Matt Chapman is my best mate. He was the best man at my wedding and the guy I can do anything with - we can sit outside talking on a patio in super trendy Southern Cali, build paper airplanes in Leeds, England and talk about comic books for hours in Dallas, Texas. I love the fact that every time he's stayed with me he shuts his eyes to go to sleep and I prepare an onslaught of fear-driven pranks to make him wet himself. Yes, the guy is my best mate. But (and it's a big but) at the end of the day we should all feel extremely lucky that Jesus was a lot more like Jesus and lot less like Mr. Matt Chapman.

Now before I go any further let me fill you in on who I am. No, I did not study at a monastery (mainly because I probably would have zero chance of keeping the whole vow of silence thing) and no, I was not trained by an underground group of Shiite Christian ninjas as much as it pains me to say that. I did however study at an incredible seminary, graduating with my Masters of Divinity and an emphasis in theology.

What all that really means is that I have been somewhat "trained" to be able to chit-chat about the deeper meanings of Scripture and it is for this reason that I am going to be bringing Gods version of the Jesus story to the table. We're going to look at why Jesus did it the way He did it, and why that is a beautiful thing that is absolutely necessary to our lives and to the world that you and I stroll around in.

Let me begin with a little bit about John the Baptist (which, I hate to disappoint the Southerners with did not just mean he went to a Baptist church) because he is evidently integral to the story. John was very much a prophet like the ones you may have heard about from the Old Testament days and he spoke with much authority. This "authority" was a big deal back then; if you or I had been in the crowd listening to John, whether we agreed with his words or not I doubt if we could have helped but listen to what he said. Mainly because he was someone who definitely "brought it" every time he spoke.

He had no problem rebuking the religious elite of his day and getting in their faces. Primarily this was because they were more concerned with their own appearances and their religious works than they were with the Lord's will for His people. By the time that we first hear about him working he had gathered a fairly large following and people from all over the region and beyond were being drawn to this extremely unique and very charismatic individual.

For John though, despite the fact that he was gathering followers and changing lives left and right he always understood and acknowledged the fact that he was simply a forerunner. He was the pre-game show, the warm-up, the opening act. His role was to prepare the way for one who was to come who would be much greater than he ever could be. One "whose sandals (he was) not fit to carry".

So despite all of John's authority, despite his powerful words and message, his extreme popularity, all his followers, etc., there was this underlying humility that had him understanding exactly what his role was and what it wasn't. He could have easily gotten caught up in himself and just how great he was at any given time but he remained a simple man (rocking that camel's hair jumpsuit, munching on some locusts, slurping down some honey) and always strived to genuinely lay the ground work for when the Savior would come.

John didn't know when this day would finally come. He didn't know when the moment would arrive when Jesus, his cousin and savior of the world would come on the scene. He also didn't know what it was going to be like. Back then there was more disagreement on what the Messiah would be like than there was on whether you had to wait 30 minutes after eating before you could go into the water and be baptized. Opinions throughout the religious world as to what this Messiah was going to bring to the table were diverse and many. Was he going to come in power? Was he going to come as a religious leader? Was he going to come and physically take over the kingdom of Rome? Was he going to bring about an entirely new kind of empire? Was he going to start a new kind of religious government? Was he going to be for separation of church and state? What was his reign going to look like?

All John had to go on was what the prophecies had said and that was what he stuck to. He had no idea when or how it would all go down.

Then that amazing day finally came. John was down at the Jordan River calling people to repentance. Upon confessing their sins they were baptized by him in the river, a sign of their sins being forgiven. He was doing what he did best and people from all over Jerusalem and Judea were coming to take part in this. It was, however, going to be a pretty big day for him.

Out of nowhere (well, from Galilee actually) Jesus came

sauntering up. John realized at that moment that this was it. This was the point that he had been proclaiming would come. Jesus was officially arriving on the scene and John was probably hoping deep down that He'd allow him to be first in line to be baptized with the Holy Spirit and with fire. He'd done his part and now it was time for him to step back and let Jesus do His thing.

But the gospels reveal that the strangest thing happened; instead of John being baptized by Jesus, the Messiah, the Son of God, the One who was infinitely more powerful than him asks to be baptized by little old John.

What?!?

This had to be somewhat of a shock to John. I mean nobody else there really knew what was going on at the time or who this guy was, but we're told that John knew. Surely of all the things that John thought might happen, this had to have been the last thing he could have expected.

So the real question about this passage is this; why on earth did Jesus, the Messiah and future Savior of Mankind come to be baptized by John, a sinful, mortal, normal guy?

To be honest, there is masses of info out there on this exact topic and you're more than welcome to go grab a commentary and study this stuff till the cows come home. Matts re-telling asked loads of questions about this scene but as we've got loads to get through I am just going lay down three main things that jump out at me, which hopefully can apply to all of our lives.

One of the first things that we take away from this, which is a more obvious and practical thing, is that by requesting to be baptized by John he was identifying Himself with John and his ministry. This may not seem like a big deal to us but it would have been huge for John. Essentially by being baptized Jesus is saying that he is on board with the message of repentance that John has been proclaiming. That He agreed with the rebuking and preaching that John had been throwing down and that He fully supported the ministry that John had been doing.

This moment links Jesus with John's ministry in a very special and powerful way; a convincing endorsement of what had been going on.

To explain a bit further I am about to be very American and use a metaphor having to do with basketball (and no, despite what Matt says, it's not just 'netball-for-men' with less people and a heavier ball). If you have trouble with this then just substitute basketball with soccer...I mean, football...and substitute Michael Jordan for some super famous, greatest-ever footballer. Now that my disclaimer is out of the way, let's get to it;

Imagine that you are running a basketball camp, but in this camp you are doing things differently than anyone has ever done them before. You are teaching skills in a way that is completely unique. You are running drills in a way that many had not seen before and are doing things differently to 'how they've always been done'. Imagine at the end of the day a lot of folks aren't really buying into the way you are doing things. Then out of nowhere, Michael Jordan (yes, the 'Air Jordan' guy) comes out to the press and says that he wants to sponsor your camp. That he wants to be a part of what you are doing and that he thinks what you are doing will change the way that the world plays basketball.

Do you think that might pull a little weight? Do you think that the world might stop and take notice?

Now change basketball camp to Johns ministry and change Michael Jordan to Jesus.

The first reason Jesus allowed John to baptize him was this; it validated Johns work.

The next thing I want to draw out is that we see that Jesus did not come on the scene the way that much of the religious culture of that day expected him to. He did not come blazing in on a fiery chariot or come in with booming trumpets and angels singing. He did not come down the road with wind blowing in his hair and a glow upon his face and He definitely did not come down to the river that day looking like what everyone thought the 'King of the Jews' would look like.

We see Jesus come as a humble man - and this is important - as a man, period. He came as the Suffering Servant that was prophesied about in the Old Testament. In this story we start to see the first glimpses of a man who came to preach the message that the "first will be last and the last will be first." He was not concerned with appearances and what the religious folks (or anyone else for that matter) might have thought of Him. He came to show us what selflessness and putting others first really looked like. He did not come to be the star of the show but rather He came to show us what the show was all about.

Lastly, and this might be my favourite bit, this story shows that Jesus came to identify Himself with us. He came into a crowd filled with dirty sinners to be baptized just like every one of them. He came down to our level, to our selfish, flawed, sinful level, and did the baptism thing just like everyone else was doing

He did not require special treatment or a separate venue. He didn't want some big announcement as to what was about to happen. He didn't request that the water be heated to hot-tub-temperature so that he could be comfortable. He was treated like everyone else. He was treated like a human being, which is what He was. And wasn't.

We see Jesus, the Son of God, linking arms with Man in the symbolic act of salvation which He himself would eventually bring about. How powerful is that?!?

This baptism was somewhat of a commissioning service from the Lord, sending Jesus out to do the ministry that God had sent Him here to do. Right from the get-go we see this powerful message of Jesus wanting us know that we can relate to Him and that we can feel confident coming to Him when we're in need.

I don't know about you but this hits home with me in a huge way. I don't know about you but when I listen to a preacher and all he talks about is how many spiritual things he's accomplished, how many times he's converted somebody sitting next to him on a plane, how deep and long his quiet times are and that he never shares any of the same struggles or weaknesses as me, I switch off. I feel like I cannot relate to them at all and that therefore they can have nothing to say to me.

Despite all the seminary stuff the truth is simple - I am not super-spiritual. I don't regularly convert strangers sitting next to me on planes and I have plenty of struggles. Me and "Captain-Super-Preacher" have nothing in common.

But if I hear a preacher talk about how badly he messed up at this point or how he blew the opportunity with this guy or about how he still struggles with such-and-such then I immediately can relate to this guy, because they sound just like me. I listen to their words, their insight and their teaching, because I figure that they must all be applicable, useful and usable by somebody like me.

Now obviously since Jesus was without sin, then He could not relate to all those folks at the river from the standpoint of their sin (even though Hebrews says He was tempted in every way, like all of us…but you'll have to read the next chapter for that bit). But (and this is the awesome part) His perfection and the fact that He could very well be sitting on a throne in the clouds next to God didn't stop Him from coming down to our level, humbling Himself and jumping into the chilly Jordan River to be baptized just like every sinful, flawed, struggling person there.

Ultimately, if you get nothing else out of everything I just said take this one thing home with you; Jesus was a real, relatable man.

Matt has one thing right in his interpretation of Jesus; He was a real man. That guy suffered. He had tough days, He struggled with losing loved ones, He went through hard times, He went through growing pains and some of the time, things didn't quite seem to work out for Him.

And yet despite the fact that He could have changed all of that in an instant, He didn't. He stayed relatable. He wasn't caught up in cute little gimmicks to impress folks. He wasn't flaunting His religion in people's faces and He wasn't acting holier-than-thou around all us sinners (even though He was). He didn't avoid getting His hands dirty with the regular folks, He wasn't sitting back in His cushy office waiting for the struggling mortals to come seek Him out and He didn't put Himself up on a pedestal. He didn't have a messiah-complex (ironic, huh?), He didn't alienate Himself from those who were different than Him and at the end of the day He stepped out of eternity to come down to our level and to give us a fighting chance.

That is a Savior I can relate to and that is who we believe that Jesus was. God in the flesh. That's a God I want to hear more about. Certainly a lot more so than one who puts on a show and says "shazam!!"

Chapter Two

Temptation in the Desert

It's easily a hundred and twenty degrees in the shade. Not that there's any shade out here, just barren rocks to stub my sandal-less toes on and enough creeping, crawling things to freak me out at every turn. Why didn't my Father...why didn't I...He...Us...make everything just look like puppies. Tiny, 8-legged, fluffy puppies. I wouldn't be creeped out and tempted to squash everything that moves if it looked up at me with the tiny eyes of a miniature Labrador.

As it is, creeping things notwithstanding, here I am in the desert. Thirty years old, sat in the sand watching my tan turn to a deep burn. I've already peeled off enough skin to make a leper jealous and my tongue keeps sticking to the roof of my mouth, making me lisp as I pray. "Father, please bring me a shhhhip of water" led to an awkward moment with a red-sea tourist barge before I managed to peel my tongue off and send them back.

To be perfectly honest, this sucks. Why I'm not on tour right now, I have no idea.

Actually I do have an idea. I know the call. I know who and what I am and where I have to go now. To put it plainly, I'm not best-pleased. For nearly 18 years now I've had to keep quiet and just get on with dads trade, all the while looking forward to the high-life of Messiah-hood. But now this. I'm as sick of this as I am of woodwork.

I'm sick of splinters. I'm sick of the smell of wood. I'm sick of early mornings, sick of hitting my thumb with a hammer and trying not to shout out my own name. I'm sick of trying to balance a chair leg while I tap nails in and then having them bend right at the last hit. I'm sick of dropping planks on my foot and of the sawdust sneezes. In short, I've been absolutely sick of this menial life and I want better for me now. I deserve better.

All my life I could have been making us a fortune. Even if I stuck with the joinery I could be carving ornate masterpieces for Herod. I could have people from Ephesus, Egypt or Ethiopia all clamoring to buy my work. I could carve wood in ways it's never been carved before (I made the platypus after all, and therefore am qualified to make any kind of weird art-form I can imagine) and could take mum quite easily out of the slums into paradise.

And yet instead I wasn't allowed. I had to wait and work. I had to sit and watch them suffer. And after all of that, after all the waiting was done I'm still not allowed to bust free. I'm here, sat on a rock getting sun burnt. Brilliant. How did this happen?!

Every single morning for the past 20 years I've had to wake up with back ache. I've felt spiders crawling across my legs in the night, even across my face sometimes. I've had to go and draw water in the dark, coughing out the dust from the street and had to try and avoid the dogs mess from next door. And when I miss it, it's in those moments - moments when the son of man, mankinds Messiah has stood in dogs mess - that I stop, look skywards and ask what on earth I am doing here.

Let's be real; in case you were unsure about this, I am God. God in the flesh. God. The God. God-in-the-bod. So how on my-green-earth did I end up here as a carpenter?!!

Let's check my resume for a moment; I'm the one who made Jupiter. In less than a day I whirled up the winds of Venus and placed Neptune where it now hurtles through its orbit. I flicked stars into space that haven't even been seen yet. I twirled my finger and cast vast supernovas, hiding them in the deepest, darkest regions of space just because I can.

I made Norway. I chiseled the cliffs of Dover with a thumbnail and ran my finger along the ground, carving out the grand canyon. I invented the properties of light and brought sound into being. I came up with the notion of gravity and, milliseconds later, decided what a duck would sound like.

I was the One who dreamt up neutrons, gauged the exact pressure of a sharks bite, poured magma into place and tapped it down with solid rock. I clicked my fingers and the laws of motion existed, tapped my foot and brought hamsters into existence then shrunk a few to make gerbils.

I forged diamonds with a finger-pinch and hid their beauty deep inside in mountains, just for the fun of it. I winked and flattened out the ocean floor, popped holes in it for conga eels and dreamed up imaginative ways for underwater creatures to mate. I made Pterodactyls, Pheasants and Phlegm and then gave man the foresight to come up with the silent "P".

I'm who decided that green was green. I chose the density of custard, made sand capable of becoming glass, compacted the mountains on Mars and rolled out the river beds of Norfolk.

I put electrons in orbit, smashed planets together, formed black holes, white dwarves and entire galaxies. And yet despite all of this, despite making every single thing in existence I still had time to make sure each and every one of Jannai-son-of-Mattathias' arm hairs were securely in place.

(In case you're wondering, Jannai-son-of-Mattathias was a boy who repeatedly pushed me into the lake as a child, holding my head under water until I gave him the figs that mum had given me. He had 14,203 arm hairs on the arm that held me under, the same number I put there at his birth.)

And yet despite all of this, despite the fact that I AM, I'm still a no one! I'm nothing! Born in a barn, hidden as a baby, forgotten as a child and put to work as a carpenter as a man. I am nothing to these people.

The other day I had to make a chair that ended up buckling under the weight of its fat owner. He wouldn't pay me for it. I felt like telling him that it was I that picked him out at birth and made the food he's evidently stuffed himself with. It was I who formed the gravity that plonked his fat behind to the floor. But instead I just had to reinforce the legs, for free. I am sick and tired of having to hold back who I really am.

Some days I watch mum trying to find some cash to pay the taxes with and I remember the moment that I came up with the consistency of gold. Without breaking a sweat I could click my fingers and turn the house itself into something Solomon would choke on his dinner at, but I didn't. I wasn't allowed. I could easily make it so that never again would I have to watch her getting thin and weak during the winter, never again would I have to lie awake thinking that tomorrow would bring with it another walk out to the workshop, another day spent chiseling out someone elses furniture with dads rusty old tools.

And you know what? It's not even just about mum. I could have saved millions by now. If I'd been born a king or a prince or even just a prophet or a Rabbi even, I could have already told people about salvation. I could have already been out there healing people. Curing illnesses and fixing paralysis. Do you know how many people perished while I sanded tables? I do.

Instead of saving the lost I've spent 30 years making shelves for ungrateful peoples kitchens and chairs for fat people.

Well this is all about to change. The baptism has started something and I'm not planning on stopping. If I'm going to have to die for these peoples sins they ought to know my name at least!! Popularity, in this faith, has always been vastly underrated but I'm going to use it for good.

And so here's where I get a bit sneaky. Here's where "he" comes in. I knew I'd have to face him before I could get started I'd just hoped it would be somewhere less hot. It's a drag and I know he'll try and cheat me, which is why I don't intend on playing fair either.

Having already waited for days I figured it was ridiculous to starve myself (especially on the brink of my big tour) so I ended up turning a couple of rocks into some roasted lamb and a nice glass of chilled wine to keep me going. After all I need all the strength I can get if I'm going to keep going at this pace for the next 3 years.

No meeting with satan is ever going to be a blast, is it? To be fair though, I already know what he's going to do. He's going to try and make me an offer I can't refuse and then try and back-stab me later on. I think my arrival has got him a bit confused and he's trying to play me. He's trying to work out his opponent, trying to gauge my defenses and my will. Well I've already know what he's going to put on the table, and I know what I'm going to do.

I'm going to accept his offer.

Stick with me here, the sun hasn't made me loopy. If I know anything about him he's going to say something along the lines of "All of the kingdoms of this world have been given to me and I'll grant you power over them if you'll just bow down to me". Well he clearly has no idea what a foolish offer he's making!

What a moron! All the kingdoms of the world if I just nod my head?!! Erm, sounds good to me! One nod and suddenly I get to rule over the world? Does he really understand what that means?! My plan is simple; I'm just going to pretend to bow down to him and then when I suddenly get given power over all of the kingdoms of the earth, imagine what I can do!

I'll start off by saving every single person in those kingdoms left, right and center. I'll heal all their sick. I'll create money for the poor. I'll bring about heaven here on earth (meaning hopefully I might not even need to die then!) and pretty soon satan will be done-for. Surely a worthy reward for simply paying lip-service to "obeying him".

He'll be ruined after that. I'll become the figurehead of every household, the focus of worship and adoration of all. I'll be the most benevolent, merciful and loving ruler this world has ever known. I'll be wiser than Solomon (and I wont let it go to my head), more influential than Moses (and I wont need the beard) and a greater king than David (and I wont scout for hot women on rooftops) and it'll be the end of satan.

No one will ever need to find out about me bowing down, and even if they did they'd surely understand that it was worth it when poverty and sickness have been abolished by my hand. Satan is a fool, and obviously hasn't thought this through at all!

I am surprised he hasn't turned up yet though, and I am getting a little peckish. A few more swan-dives off this cliff face, to get the blood pumping (it's like angelic bungee jumping, it's such a rush!) and then I'll make a spot of dinner before he arrives. Wish me luck!

JR's Response

Tiny, 8-legged, fluffy puppies, huh? Hey, I have no problem with that one at all. I am not a fan of the creepy-crawlies either and my wife is absolutely terrified of spiders so I am thinking she would totally be down for the change. I mean she loves our adorable, little Shih Tzu so if all spiders could just look like 8-legged little Brentley Rufflepuffs (don't laugh, it's her choice) then there'd be no more arachnophobia.

Regrettably this would bring up a completely different issue though. Would these new Spidtzus (spider and Shih Tzu crosses) still be dangerous and poisonous? If so then the fact that they were cuddly and cute might be even more detrimental than if they were creepy looking. I mean Brittany would go to pick one up to scratch its little belly and then before you know it the side of my wife's face would be swollen up like a cantaloupe and she'd be in the emergency room. Maybe, just maybe spiders don't look like cute, cuddly Shih Tzus for a reason.

The point being that maybe God knew what He was doing.

Now as much as I'd love to sit around and chat about how unappealing the aesthetics of insect life is and how badly those creepy crawlies need extreme makeovers, its actually our view of Jesus' interaction with satan that needs altering drastically.

Initially, Jesus didn't just randomly decide to go off on some random outing in some random location at this random time in life so that He could have some really good "me time" or maybe to try and find Himself. The Spirit that had descended upon Him at His baptism is the one who led Him to this place, at this time for a very specific reason.

Again, God knew what He was doing.

This whole "temptation in the desert" thing isn't just some sideshow attraction for the angels to sit around and observe. This isn't some after school show down between the class bully and the new kid who just happens to button his polo all the way up to the tip-top and wears his pants a little too high around his waist. This isn't even Lennox Lewis and Evander Holyfield in a Heavyweight championship bout to determine the undisputed Heavyweight champion of the world.

This is not some simple initiation for Jesus to prove His worth or a little test that Jesus has to pass to move on to the next level or anything like that. This is a gigantic and crucial moment in history. There is so much more going on here than most people gather at first glance.

Jesus is on the scene to usher in a new beginning, a new hope and a future for us all. It started with his "rebirth" at His baptism and now, in this time of temptation and testing we are going to see Jesus get it right where so many others before Him had, to put it bluntly, royally screwed up. It's all about Him having the choice to "take the easy way out". I think it'd be helpful to compare Jesus' approach with a couple of other similar examples;

Let's start with good ol' Adam, the first son of God, who was faced with a situation a lot like the one that Jesus was facing. The only difference was that his circumstances were a lot sweeter than those of Jesus. Instead of being in the desolate, horrific wilderness Adam was in this lush, perfect, everything-you-could-possibly-need Garden. And instead of having the Spirit there to guide him he actually had the God of the universe on speed dial, hanging out in the Garden with him. Not too shabby if you ask me.

Those details aside the overall occurrences of the scene were fairly identical. Adam was given instructions from God and before you know it satan shows up on the scene (in the form of some sort of talking snake. This probably should have been his first clue that all was not right).

Adam was faced with temptation and what happened? He gave in. He failed. He failed big time. He decided that he wanted to do what he thought was best as opposed to listening to God and as a result he brought death to this planet and created a separation from God. Good work Adam.

Fast forward four thousand years and lets go check out Jesus, the true Son of God. He is in the desert/wilderness (not some posh Garden) and He too has instructions from God. He too faces temptation when satan shows up on the scene and yet look at the difference in the gospel account. Jesus decides that He is going to trust the words of His Father and resist. Jesus succeeds where Adam had failed. And because of this Jesus was able to bring life to mankind and bridge the separation between God and Man.

As it says in Romans, chapter 5:18-19...

"...just as the result of one trespass was condemnation for all men, so also the result of one act of righteousness was justification that brings life for all men. For just as through the disobedience of the one man (Adam) the many were made sinners, so also through the obedience of the one man (Jesus) the many will be made righteous."

As another comparison lets look at the people of Israel. They were in the wilderness for 40 years and God had placed the Spirit upon them. We see multiple times in the book of Numbers where the Lord places the Spirit on individuals and on groups of folks such as the elders. This enabled them to carry each other's burdens, to prophesy and to better follow the Lord.

Not only does the Lord provide the Spirit but He also provided for them physically. He gave them instructions and direction and a powerful calling. But even with all this favor upon them, just like with Adam, temptation was too powerful and they couldn't adhere to the will of God. They failed as well. Although the Spirit was with them they were unable to trust its leading and follow it fully and subsequently the people of Israel missed out on God's best.

Again fast forward to Jesus. Here he is in the wilderness for 40 days and God has also placed the Spirit upon Him. He has also given Jesus instructions and a calling and yet when satan poked his ugly head around the corner, Jesus resisted temptation. He did not cave in to take the easy way out but stood strong and trusted His Father.

These moments of resisting temptation go way beyond a simple ability to follow a list of rules. Jesus is bringing hope and life to Man that had been lost for so long.

In these comparisons we see a direct ability or inability of folks being able to trust God and His word. In the unsuccessful examples we see people deciding to go with what is more appealing to them, what seems to make sense in their minds or what looks to be a more comfortable and easy road to walk down.

This is human nature, isn't it? If we have 2 options and one of them seems logical to us and a lot easier then we naturally opt for that path, don't we? I mean can you really get too upset with Adam and the Israelites for doing exactly what you (or I) probably would have done?

And yet this is where Jesus separates Himself. He doesn't go with the easy path or with the one that might seem "logical" to His human mindset. Instead He decides to purely take God at His word and fully trust that Father knows best.

When we look at each of the temptations that satan tosses Jesus' way, at the root of them all we see an undermining of God's word and His instructions for Jesus at this time. Satan is pretty flippin' crafty and he tempts Jesus with things that not only seem logical and beneficial to Him at the time but that also seem to make perfectly good sense in the larger scale of influencing mankind.

If it would have been me (or Matt) I probably would have

genuinely thought long and hard about whether I could justify taking that logical route. I would have found arguments, tried to summon up justification and reasoning behind picking the easier choice. In short, I would have crashed and burned. Jesus, however simply trusts that God's way is the best way, regardless of what to Him might seem like the logical thing to do.

In the first temptation satan tries to get the famished Jesus (who hasn't grubbed in 40 days at that point) to turn some rocks into some biscuits so that He could eat. Now in and of itself eating is not a sin. For Jesus to turn nothing into something wouldn't have been wrong - having some dinner after a long day of prayer and worship is clearly not a bad thing - but in this context it would have been. Why?

Jesus was praying and fasting to prepare Himself for the long road ahead as He knew that this was what God had planned for Him. He trusted in His mission and that God would get Him through it. Since Jesus fully believed in His Father He knew (despite his stomachs rumbling) that He would be fine without food and that God would surely provide for Him when the time was right. He did not need to take matters into His own hands, even though His hands could have easily turned those rocks and weeds into a delicious chicken korma curry, some naan and an ice cold lemonade.

The real question here was not "why wasn't Jesus allowed to make food?" it is simply an issue of trust. Did Jesus believe that God really did have His best interest at heart? Did Jesus really believe that God would get Him through the seeming starvation He was faced with? Was Jesus willing to keep going, day after day, all the while possessing the ability to feed himself but instead just trusting in Gods provision for Him? In the gospels we hear that yes, he did believe and yes, He was willing. Matt obviously places a higher priority on filling his stomach than fulfilling his calling.

The next temptation (only mentioned in Matts re-telling in the act of bungee-jumping) deals with the supernatural powers that Jesus possessed and whether He should use them or not. Satan tries to get Him to take a dive off the top of the temple and then to throw the bat-signal to the angels and have them soar on down, scoop Him up and carry Him off to safety.

Again, the simple act of Jesus doing something supernatural is, by itself not wrong or sinful. Satan knew what he was doing by posing these temptations though and I'm sure many of us can recognize his tactics. He's not making Jesus do something "evil" or even "bad". He's just making him manipulate something "good" into a way in which it's not meant to be done.

For years satan has used the same tactic with us. He can twist sex (turning something good, pure and designed by God into lust), food (turning healthiness into gluttony), zeal (tipping the balance of being passionate and committed into anger), and a multitude of other at-their-core-good emotions and events into corrupted versions of themselves. Rarely does he flat out come and tempt us to commit genocide. It's much easier for him to take something good that already exists and tweak it slightly until it's ruined. It all comes down to motive.

The fact with this temptation is that only a short while afterwards, we actually do see the angels come and attend to Jesus after satan quits messing with Him. It is not the supernatural and miraculous ability that is the issue; it is what satan was presenting to Him as a motive at that specific time that would have caused the problem.

Can you imagine what would have happened if Jesus had hurled Himself off the top of the temple in front of masses of people and then, in mid-air, sent out a command to heaven. If, all of a sudden, a crew of angelic beings fluttered on down (and let's not even get into whether you could actually see the angels or not. I mean, if the angels were invisible it would've looked like Jesus was some kind of superhero, just floating on down to the ground) and escorted Him to the earth below? What would have happened?

Simple. Pandemonium. Much like the "Jesus" in Matts interpretation He would have immediately become some circus-like attraction and people all over the place would have wanted to see more tricks and performances by "The Gravity-defying Galilean". "'Jesus The Flying Jew" would have made all the front pages. He would have gotten plenty of attention but not the kind that God had planned on.

Jesus' motives in the desert were not "playing hard to get" for His fans. He wasn't out there trying to promote controversy and build up his mysterious public image. He wasn't out for fame and He wasn't there to make a show of His power. The only public spectacle He was really planning for at that point was on a hillside

3 years from then, flanked by two other death-rowers.

So why did satan do it? Perhaps this temptation was more about satan wanting to see the extent of his enemies power. Perhaps satan was confused and concerned about what might happen if this man did start making a show or even what might happen should he try and have him killed or attacked. Satan had no idea that Jesus wasn't planning on diving from the rooftops but instead would willingly climb onto the cross. No angels would come and save him, no heavenly forces would swoop down to protect Him at that moment but satan didn't know that. Satan had no idea that He had come not to demonstrate His powers, but to die.

In the last temptation we see satan offering Jesus what might seem like the most logical, beneficial, could-be-used-for-good opportunity yet. He offers Him all the kingdoms of the world to rule and have as His own. He would be leader and ruler of everyone. As Matt suggested, just think of how much good He could do.

Just imagine all of the lives He could impact. Just try and grasp how many folks He could bring to salvation if He was in that kind of spotlight. At first glance it might seem that Matt was spot on with this one but since Jesus rejected even this seemingly logical path, then there must be something more going on here.

If Jesus was ruler of all the kingdoms of the world and in this spotlight of fame and fortune then you're probably right in thinking that He would be incredibly influential. If He was a good and benevolent ruler folks from all over the world would want to do whatever it was that Jesus would have them do.

It is this for this exact reason that God did not do it this way.

Let me explain with a little example from my own life. As far back as I can remember I wanted to be famous. Whether it was playing in the NBA as a professional basketball player, playing in the English Premier League as a professional football player or becoming a famous Hollywood actor I always had this dream of being famous.

Obviously the reasons why were simple; having plenty of money, driving absurdly expensive cars, living in an extravagant house with trap-doors and secret passage ways, being able to vacation in amazing places, being loved and adored by all my fans, and on and on and on but (honestly) there was also a very spiritual reason as well.

If I was famous and known by millions the world over then, I reasoned, imagine what kind of influence I could have on people everywhere. I could be a great Christian example to everyone out there and I could bring glory to God in so many ways because of the sheer number of people that would undoubtedly follow me. How in the world could this be a bad thing?

Well first off let me assure you that as I drove to work this morning in my car (with 273,000 miles on the clock, no air bags, cracked windshield, dents everywhere and more broken parts than operable ones) I didn't become famous. I am not exactly living the life of luxury.

As I sit here in my office at a small church in a small town in Northeast Arkansas, typing on my computer that is 6 years old and sounds like an airplane taking off I am far from this figure I dreamed about being. Sometimes I still day dream about it and yes, sometimes I still fantasize about being that person but the deal is simple (and I know that this is starting to sound repetitive); God knew what He was doing.

We all know the truth behind this and we all can surely understand why Jesus didn't take this offer if we really think about it. When you are "famous" and people follow you the truth is that you really never have any idea how many of them are following you just because you are famous or because they actually believe in you and what you're about.

Sadly enough I have seen this happen in ministry far too often. I have seen very dynamic, charismatic, influential leaders gather a large following of folks primarily because of the fact that they are pretty popular people. The problem is that as soon as they leave, change ministry, or go off elsewhere, half of the folks that they had supposedly led to Christ, end up drifting off as well.

These people had never really bought into the message that was being told they had just bought into the individual who was telling it. As soon as that individual was gone the motive for them being involved in their mission/church/ministry went as well and so they just went about their business.

This (along with the obvious complete corruption that would have happened in a heartbeat) is why I will never be famous. It won't help God or my ministry.

This is also exactly the issue that God wanted to avoid with Christ. He did not want the world to buy into the Gospel because Jesus was this mega-famous ruler or because He could do all these cool tricks. Pretty soon those tricks would be gone and even as a ruler He would one day die.

God wanted the world to be changed because of His message of salvation and He wanted the message to be presented simply, clearly and without all the bells and whistles. That way when people did choose to follow and live life for Christ it would have to be for the right reasons. Yes, they would have recognized something in Christ that was amazing, outstanding, remarkable even. But that recognition would merely shunt them towards His message, His way of life, His sacrifice and ultimately towards their redemption in his death.

Perhaps there was a reason that Jesus was so normal. A carpenter. Born in a shack in the corner of a remote village to an unknown girl. Thirty years of woodwork as his background. No power, no prestigious friends, no kings or rulers on speed dial. Perhaps there was a reason He was so ordinary – because his message was anything but.

Everything about Jesus' life points towards God and towards His message of salvation to a lost world. Jesus came as a servant and as a sacrifice not as a showman.

So perhaps we're beginning to see why this time for Jesus on temptation-island was about so much more than just some simple tests that needed to be checked off before He could move on. In this story we see the depths of what it means to truly trust God and His word, even though it may appear sometimes that by doing it another way might make life more comfortable. That while a different and easier path might be more beneficial, might not even be "sinful" necessarily, it simply would not be what God has called us to do and that is the bottom-line. We, like Jesus, have to trust that God's best way is way better than our best will ever be.

And this is where we fail far too often. We hear what God has to say about sin and about how to live our lives but for some reason we continue to think that doing it our way makes a little more sense. So what happens is that we go off and do it our way and if it fails we fall flat on our face, we get hurt, and then we come to our senses (for a little while at least) and come running back to God.

Unfortunately this normally only lasts...well, it only lasts until the next temptation comes along that seems to lead us down another easy and logical path that seems to make such great sense to us. And then we're off again, trying to do things the way we think is best.

It's a horrific cycle that, sadly enough, most of us have been through far too often. Or perhaps we're in the middle of right this second. If that's the case then maybe what we need to do is look to Jesus and see how He dealt with it. We need to let go of "our way of dealing with it" and start trusting God, even when we have the best intentions.

Now, lastly, aside from this huge (and even "huge" might be an understatement) issue of trusting God we see that all over this story there is another powerful reason behind why this temptation tale should mean so much to us.

If you recall from the last chapter one of the most important things we saw in the baptism of Jesus was the fact that He was a real man and, because of this He immediately became an example of someone we could all relate to.

For me, more than anything else in the story of His temptation the fact that He is 100% human being, just like you and me, gives me hope beyond hope when temptation comes our way. At his core Jesus was not able to resist temptation just because He was the Son of God or because He was God-in-the-flesh or because He had some heavenly ace up His sleeve.

No, He was able to resist temptation because He knew what the Word of God said, because He trusted that God knew best and because He made the choice to not give in.

We all can do this. Jesus showed us that we have the ability to stand toe-to-toe, face-to-face with satan and overcome. When the enemy gets in our grill we too have a choice. We can resist him. We can say no and we can win. I only know that that's true because Jesus – the man – showed me so.

This is something that isn't often told in churches. Personally, I think it should be screamed from the rooftops. Hear this loud and clear; we can be victorious over the enemy. How am I so sure? The bible tells me so, and Jesus shows me so.

"Resist the devil and he will flee from you".

There it is in black and white. If you haven't heard it or don't believe it, chances are that he's already showing you an easier path to take; giving up or giving in. But the truth is that we do not have to be chained to our struggles and our sin any longer. Jesus has showed us that we can do this and he, unlike us, could have squished satan like a bug. Instead he resisted. You and I can too.

We have the choice every day to either listen to God or to ourselves. To resist or give in. Satan is not unstoppable and our temptation is not unbeatable. Read 1 Corinthians 10. Read the gospels; temptations can be overcome.

Whatever you are going through, this story is relevant. If you think that what you're facing is only small-fry remember that Jesus resisted making bread. If you think that your temptations are too large remember that Jesus resisted displaying his heavenly power to mankind and thereby effectively preventing his execution. And if you think that somehow by you giving in, in some twisted way, you can glorify God remember that Jesus resisted ruling the world in order to pick up the cross.

There's the simple truth. Be bold, make the wise choice and follow Jesus' examples.

Funnily enough Jesus faced echoes of these temptations only pages on from where they're written down. Jesus goes and feeds the 5000, making bread out of nothing. He faces a palm-tree-laden entry into Jerusalem with peoples voices lifting him up as "The King". Finally he faces the garden of Gethsemane and the challenge of allowing himself to be captured, tortured and crucified with armies of angels probably straining at the leash, simply waiting for the command to come and save Him.

And what happens? His perseverance and practice at resisting temptation carries on. Yes, He makes the bread but gives glory to God for it. He rebukes those who follow him just for a free dinner, carrying on the "man shall not live by bread alone" message for

43

the lost.

He knows that those people crying out "King" will soon be shouting "Kill". He knows that his mission is for the cross, not the crown. Yes, He fulfills the prophecy and enters Jerusalem that way but it doesn't go to His head. He carries on the "You shall…serve Him only" line, knowing where His service will lead.

And finally He doesn't call for angelic assistance. He doesn't "test" God. He gives up His right to heavenly bodyguards and allows himself to be killed.

So at the end of all of this we see two glaring points staring us in the face. The first message is simple; trust God, period. He knows best and you can count on that. Do not think for a second that you're going to find a loophole, that you're going to do it your way one time and then God is going to be like, "well, looky there! I never would've thought to do it that way but it sure worked out better. Well done, my good and faithful servant, you've taught me something! Guess its true what y'all say; you learn something new every day." That, sadly, is just not going to happen.

The other message is the simple fact that you can choose to avoid temptation, to not give in to sin and to not let satan keep boxing you in the grill. You can choose to ask Christ to break you free from those chains that have bound you to your junk for ages and you can be a conqueror. Jesus, as a 100% human and as a real man showed us that it's possible and gave us the weapons to do it with.

Temptation is not un-conquerable. Jesus did it and he was the same bones and blood as you and me. He had access to heavenly powers but didn't use them. Instead he chose to simply obey Gods word and trust in His help. We should too.

Chapter Three
Choosing the Disciples

Well, satan never showed up. I guess my Father must have stepped in somehow. Trudging back to town I started trying to piece together a few ideas about the new team I needed to assemble. I cannot do this alone. Seriously, how can I be the front man and also sort out the venues, make bookings, arrange meals, clean sandals and deal with autograph hunters? I need a stage-crew. I need some backup.

I'd already got some names in my head by the time I'd passed Jerusalem so I figured I'd simply be bold and go and visit them. Ask them to follow me. Detail them the life I could offer them – a life of packed out shows, of fame and fortune, of adoring groupies and of free lunches. I'd sell them the package. I figured once they were on board and signed up to their contracts we'd then sit down and hammer out the major issues. Come up with a shared vision and have some training input on administration matters (how to cast out demons and heal the sick, measurements for their matching uniforms etc.) and then arrange who makes the tea.

Here's how I figured it; this team would need to be more than just a group of followers. These guys would need to be icons. Role Models. These men will be the "Saints" of mankind-to-come. With this in mind then, I asked myself one simple question; who would believers want as their poster-boys? Who would they want up on their walls as great examples of holy men? Simply put, who would Christians in centuries to come want to look at, trust and believe in as examples of my new kingdom? These men were set to be legends so I couldn't take just anyone.

This was going to be a unique job offer. These guys were going to hold the keys to heaven in their hands. They were going to be my ambassadors, my mouthpieces and my pale reflections on earth. For generations to come these were going to be the guys who set the foundations of my following. They would be messengers of my mission and spokesmen of my offered salvation.

Mind you, as I did some blue sky thinking and thrashed out an outline for the job description I realized that as a fledging start-up-mission this might actually be a harder sell than I first thought. Sure fame would come but kicking through the sand I started coming up with quite a startling rough job advert for the role;

Self employed joiner / wine-making-entrepreneur / savior of mankind seeks like minded individual for unique job opportunity in the public sector. Candidates should have a wide-grasping knowledge of scripture, an awareness of the prophecies and their fulfillment and most importantly be without sin.

Previous experience in demon casting, snake handling and crowd control is desirable but not essential. Must have own transportation and be self-reliant (post is voluntary, un-paid and comes with a high chance of social stigmatism attached). Must be willing to commit to a 3-year contract, at the end of which termination is a probable option.

Perks include all the fish, bread and wine you can stomach plus the chance to have future generations of parents name their children after you. Potential publishing deal for your memoirs is also an option.

This post presents the lucky candidate with the opportunity to experience the wide-ranging cultural diversity of Palestine as the chairing of focus groups, seminars and speaking arrangements with all major religious and racial groups will be another part of the role. An awareness of both Roman and Jewish judiciary law may also be a desirable key asset in a candidates resume. The candidate should also be adapt at crisis management, negotiation and conflict resolution.

Those interested must be young, talented go-getters with the drive and tenacity needed to overcome any obstacle (opposing authorities, angry crowds, probable state-endorsed-execution) in order to pass on the vision of their manager to others.

Applications in scroll-form should be sent to Mr. J. Christ, C/O

The Desert, etc.etc.

Hmmm. This truly was going to be a tough sell.

The trouble is that I cant have just any Tom, Dick or Thaddeus off the street. It'd be easy enough to get anyone of the dock hands or tax collectors to follow me with a few cheap parlor tricks but I need people who won't let me down when the going gets tough and the magic dries up. I need people with public speaking experience and with that inner spark that ignites others passions. I need warriors and people who could act as my body guards when the crowds get rowdy. I need people who others will look at and say "wow this guy is amazing! Let's follow him…towards God, of course". I don't have time to nurture talent or to grow skills. I only want to choose people who already have what it takes.

The shortlist of candidates was, well, short. With all the traits that I needed up front in my followers there were only a precious few that were good enough to make the cut.

My first stop was easy. Ducking under the smaller archway the temple opened up into a cobbled courtyard, the far end of which was currently filled by bodies, all huddled over in deep discussion.

Approaching, I called out his name and waited as the throng fell silent. Gradually, majestically the huge frame of a man rose up from the middle of them, his robes spilling down his massive back. The blue borders of his garments were immensely thick, the broad phylacteries far more broad and…phylacteryish…than his counterparts. Truly trumpets should have been playing as this man stood up. This was Peter.

There was little doubt in my mind; here was my rock. This man-mountain would be the center-piece of my back-up-band. He'd be the prop of my fledgling church and the backbone of my body of believers.

They called him "Honest Peter" and I'd heard of his reputation even as a younger man. Immensely wise and incredibly learned in the scripture, he was as strong in debate as he was in physique. He had no rival throughout all the Pharisees and Sadducees. Trained at an early age to memorize scripture, he was taught to unwrap the law and to keep himself morally upright. From all the stories it was clear that he was as near to perfection when it came to his personal dedication and faith as could be.

If there was one man that I'd be happy stamping my name on it'd be this guy. He could provide the moral core and remind others of the ethical code I was going to teach. He could lead my people and most importantly provide the academic back-up to my words. As a carpenter I have no validity. Except in him.

I know for a fact that my words are going to be studied, pored over and have their verification sought. People are going to pull sentences apart and tear open meanings in even the smallest phrases of what I say, so who should I have standing on my shoulder? Someone who cant even read or write?!! Someone that no one has ever heard of? May it never be!

I need a scholar. I need a learned man. I need someone who others will look at and think "right, well if he's obviously ok with what this guy is saying maybe I should be too." Peter is that man, no question about it.

For my next target I headed to the outer walls, out towards the lepers. I had heard rumors of this fellow back when I was banging nails in Nazareth. Born from a vastly rich family but convicted of his duty to serve others he comes out of his mansion and travels out of the city limits daily to minister to the poor and sick.

Trained as a doctor and scientifically sound, Andrew already has a reputation in the city as one of the few truly humble "good" men around. Selfless, loving, caring and giving; this man would be the beating heart of my new group. After I had healed people he'd be able to do the follow up sessions, the check-ups and the "pastoral" stuff. I simply am not going to have the time to follow up on any of the people I heal and someone needs to take the time to counsel them, to explain what's just happened to them and to rehabilitate them fully. It's bad management to not follow up on a salvation moment. We need to hand out cards and take contact details, transcribe stories and take detailed accounts of miracles. Andrew has the heart for that kind of ministry.

Who's going to look after the demon possessed, once I drive their spirits out? Who's going to take the time to teach the lame how to run again? Who's going to monitor the previously-blinds eye-sight? Andrew is who.

If I'm honest it also won't hurt that he's filthy rich as well. We're really going to need some cash-flow if this mission is going to hit the big time. Staged events, planned shows, mission retreats; these all cost money (even though obviously we'll take donations afterwards, just to cover our costs of course) and in that respect, Andrew is our cash-cow. I had thought about just converting Herod and being done with it but the whole "marrying your brothers wife" thing really put a damper on that. Plus he'd just hog the spotlight. So Andrew it is - my "good man" with the big wallet.

And then lastly I need a hypocrite. Literally, I need a "Hypocrite", what the Greeks have been calling these stage actors I keep seeing on the street corners. I need someone with some public speaking experience, someone with a sense of performance about them and most importantly someone who can work a crowd.

I spotted John a while back as the lead in some awful tragedy they were enacting. A great looking guy with instant charm and likeability I knew right there and then that this was a face that could sell a thousand replica crucifixes.

The way I see it, without being too blunt is this; there is little point having ugly, quiet people in this band-of-brothers. Don't get me wrong, they can be in the church. They can perform many valuable tasks for my kingdom and they are more than welcome to attend any event I run. The "body of Christ" will always need gall bladders and pancreatic organs. Hidden, odd-shaped or weird looking things that quietly just go about getting the job done. But my body also needs a mouth and it helps if it has all its own teeth. John will take that role.

People will listen to him and people will come to hear us all if he's there. He's popular with the crowds, popular with the ladies and can bring in an attendance. Without a doubt, he's in.

And really, that's it!

I don't want a big stage-crew. With more people there's always more chance of someone messing about, screwing something up or back-stabbing you if you trust your vision to them. There's always the risk that they might get off-message, might make a mistake, and then who does it all fall back on? Me.

No, for this venture I plan on keeping it tight. Keep your friends close, your wealthy, wise and attractive friends closer and anyone who works with fish where they belong. In a boat.

Association is everything; I don't want people to see me with idiots as co-workers. I don't want freaks, weirdoes, geeks, dorks, sinners or anyone who smells of trout working alongside me. I'll happily love them, help them and speak to them but I don't want them in my inner circle. People should aspire to be better and that'll only happen with inspirational people in my following.

I'm also handing over the keys of heaven to these men. I'm placing the future of mankinds salvation into their palms. The hands that grasp this amazing gift shouldn't be callused with boat ropes and cut with fish bones. The gift is too expensive to be wasted on that sort.

So that's it; Peter, Andrew and John are going to be my men.

These are my disciples, these are my fishers of men. And so it begin

JR's Response

Looks like this is going to be a tough one. I hate to admit it but the above train of thought makes pretty good sense on the surface. I mean, if Jesus did hope to save the world and He only had a limited time to do just that then why not select the best of the best, the cream of the crop or the religious elite of the day??

It's a legitimate question...

Selecting the super spiritual, religious icons of the day makes perfect logical sense so why on earth did Jesus not only NOT select an incredibly holy, all-star squad as His disciples but instead choose a group of folks who were just about the complete opposite?!

Again, a legitimate question...

When we really stop and think about it it's definitely hard to grasp the reasons behind Jesus' choices at first glance. His disciples were going to play a crucial role in how His entire mission would play out. They were going to be Jesus' right hand men. They were going to be the ones who were going to implement His vision, who were going to lift His banner and who would be the ones to carry the torch after Jesus was gone. It would seem sensible then that these would have to be folks who were on top of their game in every way possible.

Perhaps, to try and understand Jesus' decisions it'd help to look at what it really meant to be someone's "disciple".

Back in Jesus' day as a disciple you were much more than just a student. You were more than just a pupil of a particular rabbi. You were more than just some gopher who went and made copies and

ran errands for the busy old teacher. You were more than just a parrot who recited what the master taught and preached about. You were more than just a publicist who got the message out about what this particular leader thought and believed.

In general if you were a disciple you were well educated, extremely bright, well versed in scripture and you were wholeheartedly committed to what your rabbi said and did.

And most remarkably as a disciple you were someone that your rabbi believed in.

If you were chosen to be a disciple then the rabbi believed with all his heart that someday it could be you that carried on his legacy for generations to come.

This was much more than a simple teacher/student relationship.

So with all this being said and given all the criteria of what a traditional disciple looked and acted like we again return to the problem of Jesus' choices. It is almost baffling when we stop and consider what was at stake for Him and then look at who Jesus put His faith and trust in.

Let me draw a simple analogy for the squad of disciples that Jesus opted to go with;

I absolutely love soccer (yes, I am American and I know that it is 'football' to the rest of the world but I grew up calling it soccer so just relax) and as I'm writing this the World Cup has just finished (which saddens me as now I have to wait another four years to see if my country can do any better).

Anyways let's just say, hypothetically that I am the greatest soccer player in the world (and not merely on FIFA on the Xbox) and that I have to handpick the players who will play along side of me in the next World Cup, in Brazil, in 2014.

While we're in imagination land let's also just say that for some reason I can actually select anybody in the world to be on my team and not just American folks. Also because I am undeniably the best player in the world anybody I ask to play on this dream team of soccer super stars will say yes in a heartbeat.

Now immediately, if you are a soccer fan on any level you are probably already starting to process in your mind who you would choose to be on this team. You are probably thinking about who the best keeper in the world is, who the best defensive players are, the best midfielders, the best strikers, etc.etc.

Chances are that no matter which soccer-fan you might talk to there would end up being a lot of the same names thrown around in this discussion. For keeper; Julio Cesar, Iker Casillas, and Buffon. Defensively we could throw around the names Ferdinand, Sergio Ramos, Puyols, Vidic, and Maicon. As far as midfielders, we could go with Messi, Gerrard, Landon Donovan (got to show some love for my country) Kaka, Xavi, and Cristiano Ronaldo. And then with forwards we could list Rooney, Luis Fabiano, David Villa, Klose, Drogba...the list could go on and on.

We could discuss, debate, and chat about this all-star squad for hours on end but at the end of the day I imagine that the final 11 would be fairly similar across the board, drawn from the universally recognized 'best-players' worldwide.

It'd be common-sense to assume that you probably wouldn't see any names on the list (or even in discussion) that aren't currently playing with some of the top clubs in some of the top leagues in the world. You probably wouldn't see any names listed that aren't currently playing for their national team. And obviously you definitely wouldn't see any names listed that aren't currently busy playing professional soccer!

So then with all that being said let's say as I begin to select my dream team, the team that I think will come along side of me to give America the best chance on the planet to win the World Cup in 2014, that I don't select any names off the list we just chatted about. I don't pick Messi, I don't pick Casillas, I don't pick Sergio Ramos, I don't pick Drogba and I don't even pick hometown hero Donovan. Instead of all of those names, with my first pick I select Steve Bookerson.

Yes, that's right, Steve Bookerson. You all know Steve, right?!

Steve Bookerson, 29, plays soccer for "Jonesboro United", an average team in the men's recreational league here in town. Obviously he doesn't get paid for playing and so he supplements his income by stacking shelves at the local supermarket. To be fair though he does have a decent amount of skill. I mean he did win M.V.P of the league...ten years ago.

So there's 'ol Booky. Steve's in my starting line-up. After all, as the chant goes, there's only one...Steve Bookerson.

Then it's on to my next selection and again I look right past Rooney, Buffon and Vidic and I go with that crowd favourite...Jake Batson.

Jake is a local high school Math Teacher. Yes, he may be 36 but hey, he played soccer growing up and even played in a club up until high school before deciding to switch to basketball and play that in college instead. But, after failing to make it professionally, he gave up the dream of being a sportsman and decided to just go back to his hometown and be a teacher.

After Steve and Jake, I skip right on past Puyols, Ronaldo, Gerrard and Villa and I select the ever-exciting Chase Gilmore.

Mr. Gilmore plays music at a nearby church, is only 22 and no, he's not what you'd call a "soccer player". Or even what you would call "coordinated" most of the time. Sometimes over the years he's been dragged into kick-abouts with friends but generally what goes through his mind doesn't quite make it all the way to his feet and before he knows what's happened the other team is running the other way with the ball. He is definitely one who should keep his day job.

Now I could keep doing this until I had listed an entire squad but I think you probably get the gist of the point I am trying to make.

First and foremost it would be pretty nuts to build an all-star soccer team and not include any of the names I listed, any of the world-famous players.

Secondly it would be completely absurd to select a soccer team that didn't even have any professional soccer players on the team.

Thirdly, it'd be crazy to include players who don't currently...play soccer.

But then on top of that it would be <u>absolutely ludicrous</u> to select anyone who can't even kick a ball!

If we were compiling lists, including these names would immediately lose me any credibility that I had as a soccer player or as someone who had any clue whatsoever as to who would be needed to make a good team.

If the ridiculousness of this example makes any amount of sense to you at all then you can maybe begin to see how seemingly crazy it was for Jesus to have selected the folks that He chose.

So was Jesus crazy to select the team he ended up with? Did his choices reflect his lack-of-knowledge regarding the serious call of discipleship?

The truth is that Jesus didn't just pick the first 12 guys He stumbled upon. He didn't call up Rabbi Bernstein and ask for 12 guys from his class. He didn't select the first 12 applicants to the

"Jesus School of Discipleship". He didn't eeny-meeny-miny-moe His way down the street until He came up with 12 solid individuals.

No, Jesus chose who He chose with intentionality and purpose.

To be completely honest we don't know exactly how He selected who He selected but we do know that He chose who He chose for a reason - actually, for a lot of reasons but I am just going to point out a few;

First of all we don't have to look too far in His selections to see that His entire crew is filled with <u>regular guys</u>. Various jobs are represented in this small group of folks but none of them are particularly prestigious or notable to the society around them. For the most part, these are just normal, hard-working guys. They aren't professional church folk and yet Jesus chooses them to be some of the most significant "church folk" in the history of mankind.

This simple truth tells us a huge amount about Jesus' priorities regarding discipleship. Jesus doesn't need the best of the best. He calls regular folks and wants to use these regular folks to do anything-but-regular things.

Without singling anyone out, would any of you out there reading these words right now consider themselves part of the 'B' team? Part of the not-good-enoughs? Part of the uneducated, part of the didn't-go-to-seminary group, part of the don't-have-a-degree crew, part of the don't-work-at-a-church crowd or part of the terrified-to-get-up-in-front-of-anyone-and-speak gang? Has anyone out there always kind of thought that they just weren't cut out to be an influential kind of person?

In fact while I'm asking questions, how many of you would just consider yourself one of life's 'regular folks'? Perhaps, because of that, maybe you've not felt as if you can do a whole lot for God compared to the amazing-church-folk around you? I mean that's *why there are pastors, youth ministers, chaplains and missionaries, right? God chose <u>those folks</u> to do the ministry so that all you have to do is head to church every now and then and just keep quiet. You're not cut out for changing the world...that's <u>their</u> job, right?!*

Well guess what??

Jesus called people like you.

I think most of us fall into the 'regular-folk' category in some way or another. I think that most of us if we are completely honest with ourselves would come to the conclusion that if Jesus only calls those who are (in the worlds terms) bright enough, educated enough, well-off enough, talented enough, charismatic enough or good enough then we wouldn't make the grade. We wouldn't get in the gang. He simply would never choose someone like us, not with the other choices out there. We don't match-up.

But here is where Jesus' selection of His disciples should bring you back to reality. Jesus chooses some dock-workers, some fishermen with no evangelism training to go and preach the Gospel to all the nations. He chooses a tax collector with no medical skills whatsoever to go and heal the sick. People with fish guts on their hands are told to cast out demons and ordinary laborers are tasked with saving the worlds lost.

So basically, to cut a long story short, if you think you're unqualified and not cut out to follow Jesus then that is really the only qualification required.

If you're feeling extra "regular" right now then Jesus says to you "Come and follow me". The calling He made to His disciples was a reflection of the calling He makes to us;

He chose folks that were far from perfect and who needed a lot of guidance and hand-holding along the way because <u>we</u> are far from *perfect and need quite a bit of hand-holding.*

He chose folks who He knew would fail and drop the ball because He knows that <u>we</u> are regularly going to fail and drop the ball.

He chose folks who had limited gifting's and who would have to rely on Him entirely because He knows that we all have limited gifting's and that <u>we will need to rely on Him entirely</u>.

He chose folks who worked in regular jobs, doing regular things, just to get by.

He chose folks who "religious" people would most likely judge, scoff at and think they were too good for.

He chose imperfect, scared, flawed, and weak individuals, normal-humans, real-men, tax-payers, earners and average-joes.

Are you beginning to see the picture? Jesus is a fan of normal people. God can and will still use people like <u>us</u>. Being a "regular" guy really has nothing whatsoever to do with the amazing, incredible, life-changing and completely <u>irregular</u> feats that God can use you to accomplish.

Looking throughout Scripture, this pattern continues;

Moses was a shepherd,

David, a sheep herder,

Jesus was a carpenter,

Matthew, a tax collector,

Luke, a doctor,

Paul was a tent-maker...

Do you see it?

These were regular folks (Jesus the obvious exception) with regular jobs just living regular lives and yet God used them to do extremely irregular things.

Once again, Jesus shows us just how important it is to realize that there is nothing wrong with just being a regular guy.

In the chapter on baptism Jesus shows us that he got baptized just like a regular guy. In the temptation chapter, Jesus is tempted by satan just like a regular guy. And here Jesus chooses to walk, side-by-side with folks who were just regular guys.

We live in a world where status is everything. Those who we give platforms of leadership to or who we allow to speak have to have certain credentials, accolades, references, etc. Certainly in our churches we respect the best and the brightest and expect that those in power - and certainly those who lead us - are the cream of the crop.

And yet somehow I have a feeling that God, through Jesus, showed us that these things aren't all that important. Perhaps it was so we could all relate to them or perhaps it was so that their amazing deeds were clearly only His doing. For whatever reason His rule was simple;

The more regular, the better.

Jesus' choice of disciples shows that God can use you, no matter what. Perhaps it's time for you to put your insecurities aside and realize that the reason Jesus did it the way He did it was to show the world that He can and will use you regardless of how regular you might be.

This was a team filled with Steves, Jakes and Chase's...a team of nobodies.

Jesus didn't select the elite, He didn't select the movers and shakers. He didn't select the ultra devout, and He didn't even select the committed role players. Jesus chose folks who weren't even on the radar.

He chose an uneducated, rough-around-the-edges and far-from-perfect group of folks to walk by His side and attempt to change human history and that is far more significant than a World Cup title (well...at least it is to some).

Now for the next reason why Jesus chose who He chose.

When we look at the very beginning of His ministry and who He selected first, what were they busy doing when He chose them? Don't think too hard on this one; literally, what were they doing?

They were working. They had jobs. They were most likely practicing their family trade. This might not seem too significant to you but it is very significant if you know a little bit about education in the Jewish culture.

In their culture the kids would start going to school at a very young age and began learning all about their Jewish religion. They would start by memorizing the Torah and those who couldn't keep up simply wouldn't make the cut.

Any children who were remaining would move on to memorize the whole Old Testament which obviously would weed out another large number of kids. The number of students remaining would rapidly get less and less.

After this they would progress into rigorous training about what the Old Testament said, what it taught, different translations and lots of other deep, spiritual matters. This hard discipline sifted out further wheat from the chaff and left only those who were dedicated enough to be willing to do everything they could to possibly become one of the rabbi's disciples.

This was the hope of every kid and of every parent. To be asked to become a disciple of a local rabbi was an honor that nothing else could compare to. You were definitely classed as one of the spiritual elite if that happened.

Now back to our disciples. If they were busy working out in the real world then does that mean they were disciples of a local rabbi or not?

And if they weren't disciples of a local rabbi then do you think they made it through the rigorous religious training?

And if they didn't make it through the rigorous religious training and couldn't quite memorize all those numbers in Numbers and all those weird laws in Leviticus then do you think it's entirely possible that some of them didn't even make it through the first round of cuts?

The sad reality is that at some point in all of these disciple's lives they had the same single experience of the religion of their day – a religion that they were brought up to love more than anything – when it looked them in the eyes and told them they weren't good enough.

"I'm sorry John but you're just not what we're looking for."

"You know James it looks like you're just not cut out for this."

"Peter, it's ok...not everyone can be a part of this."

"Andrew you're great guy but we're just going in a different direction and we're not going to need you."

Every single one of them had probably felt the sting of being told that they just weren't spiritual enough, smart enough, religious enough or well-versed enough to be a disciple. All of them had taken that long walk home after being told that they weren't cut out to be one of the special ones.

How many of these guys do you think were turned-off religion completely after this? How many of them do you think felt burned by the church? How many of them do you think saw God in a different light because of this experience as a child?

Let me ask a different question - How many of you out there have been burned by "the church" and have been completely turned off to religion because of something that happened to you along the way?

"I'm sorry you cannot attend this service because of what you're wearing."

"I'm sorry you cannot belong to this church until you check off this to-do list of religious accolades."

"I'm sorry you can't lead this small group or teach this class because of who you spend your time with on the weekends."

"I'm sorry I don't really think you are cut out for ministry."

Any of those sound familiar?

The Church will always be imperfect because it is filled with "us", a bunch of imperfect people. Because of this there will always be people out there messing up Jesus' calling. The key is to look at Jesus' priorities, not theirs.

Jesus didn't just accept those who'd had a problem or a gripe with the church, He actively called those very people to be His disciples. These were the ones He built His own church upon.

These were His rocks, His founding fathers. The message is simple; don't let your personal baggage with religion get in the way of realizing that Jesus is still calling people like you to go out and follow Him.

And now for the last reason why He chose who He chose.

Jesus is pretty smart. I'm pretty sure that's a given. But the deal is that He's so smart that He knows what we are like and knows the situations we will get ourselves into. He knows that if we are going to be in religious circles all the time the chances are that some days we'll mix with folks who we kind-of-don't-like.

I hate to say it but even as a follower of Christ you're probably not going to like every single human being you come in contact with. Chances are that you might even have some disagreements with folks or have some personal grievances with them. What on earth is one to do?!

Here is where the genius of Jesus' choice of disciples comes in, yet again.

Let me try and explain...

Many of the disciples were fishermen. That was the job that they did to provide for their families and to put food on the table and, despite its lowly status, they could actually make a fairly decent living out of it.

One of the frustrations that all the fishermen had was the issue of taxes. They each had to pay a tax, based upon the fish that they caught. This was frustrating because it took hard-earned money out of their pockets, sometimes food (literally) right off their table and, as there was little structure or legislation protecting them, a lot of the time the tax collectors would just tax whatever they felt like taxing.

As long as Caesar got his share then the tax collector could up the charge to whatever he felt like so that he could put some extra coin into his own pocket.

Needless to say, fishermen and tax collectors were not the best of friends, in fact, some would say that the fishermen despised these shady tax-men.

So, what does Jesus go and do?

He calls four or five fishermen to be His disciples and then before you know it, Jesus calls in a nice little tax collector.

Do you think there might have been a little tension there?

Do you think those fishermen might have been a little upset at the fact that Jesus invited this shady tax collector to be part of their little gang?

You know full well that this would have been extremely difficult for these guys to stomach at first, but, as I've said, Jesus was smart. He knew what He was doing.

The Gospel message is one of reconciliation. It is a message that breaks down all borders, all barriers, all genders, all races and any little personal conflicts that might exist. When we look at these disciples we see from the very beginning that Jesus was teaching them what this 'Good News' was all about, and how hard it could be to put into practice. Just by the make-up of their group, He was saying that they were going to have to learn a lot about grace, forgiveness, and unconditional love, just to get along and function as disciples.

They were in for quite the adventure.

It is unlikely that whatever church you may be in is full of perfect people, who all get along perfectly, doing perfectly well at loving each other...perfectly. Chances are that there are some people who rock the boat, push you out of your comfort zone, or who simply you don't like.

Jesus says, right from the start, that if we're to be people who outwardly spread His message of love and reconciliation, we had better practice it internally as well. The disciples were a mixed bunch, who could have easily split up from their prejudices. Instead, they put Christ's words into practice, and became the original disciples.

If they can do it, so should we.

We simply can never expect the world to take Jesus' words seriously if we're seen as divisive and broken within our own church walls. If the local people had seen the disciples gossiping about Matthew, quarrelling and fighting amongst themselves, what would they have thought about Jesus?

And what more did it say about Him, when they didn't?! When people saw these previous enemies getting on and loving one another?!

So there we go. What appears to be this seemingly simple process, where Jesus basically selects some buddies to go with Him on a mission trip, is actually far more complex a situation.

Like I said, Jesus isn't a fool, choosing the first followers he came across out of the need for some company. He intentionally chose those 12, and in so doing, He made a gigantic statement for us all to hear;

He chose regular folks. He specifically chose folks that we all can relate to. He chose folks just like you and me.

He chose folks who had been burned by religion because He knows that many of us have been or will be burned as well.

He chose folks who didn't really get along because He <u>knows</u> that we will always come across folks we don't really get along with and yet we're still called to do ministry with them.

Essentially, in choosing the disciples that Jesus did, He is saying loud and clear, to everyone on the planet;

"Now there can be no excuses. I don't care where you come from or where you've been. I don't care if you finished high school or not. I don't care if you can speak well in front of a large crowd or cant. I don't care what you do for a living. I don't care if you got picked last in gym class. I don't care if you've failed to become part of the religious elite in your hometown. I don't care if "church" has burned you more times than you can count. I don't care if you don't really get along with some of the folks at the church down the street. I don't care how insignificant you think you are...because all that matters is that <u>I think you're significant</u> and I believe you can do incredible things, by My side. So come on and follow me."

If you're a regular guy or gal, then Jesus has just shouted out your name...come on down!

Chapter Four
The Parable of the Prodigal Son

I cannot believe the pandemonium here. People are queuing around the block, the crowds are pressing in from all sides and the noise! The noise is ludicrous! And everyone's here to see me!

It started out quietly enough; me in the centre healing a few easy ones (headaches, nosebleeds, no show-stoppers) until I started to feel the bodies crushing in around me and so I took to the mountain side.

The crowd fell silent, all eyes were on me. I knew I needed to ease them in gently to what I was about to say. I'd practiced some opening gags earlier on in the evening with the disciples who'd laughed and roared at my jokes (even if I did catch them rolling their eyes afterwards) so I felt ready. I was prepped, my cue cards were colour-coded and in order. This was my first, proper teaching session;

"Now then ladies and gents, how is everyone? Anyone in from Nazareth? Any Galileans?! Hmmm…I thought we might have priced you guys out?! Just kidding, just kidding.

Anyways, before we get down to business let me ask you this; Why did people say that Boaz was mean before he got married? Anyone?!! Because he used to be RUTH-LESS!"

(Pause for laughter and applause. Not as much as I'd hoped but I press on.)

"And who was the greatest financial mind in Egypt? No? No one? Pharaohs daughter. Why? Because she went down to the Nile and collected a little prophet!"

(Since when has there been this many crickets out in the daytime?)

"And lastly, before we really get started here; how do we know that men made the coffee in Israel and not women?

Because they're all HE-BREWS!!!"

Yes, ok, on hindsight the Pharisees, the lame, the sick and the lepers aren't the ideal crowd for observational comedy. Ignoring the few coughs and tumbleweed response I carried on though, reading directly from my cards;

"Ah but enough of this hilarity, let's get down to business…"

My disciples started humming a low gospel theme behind my words, rising and falling perfectly in pitch to the emotions I purveyed.

"I'm not here to mess you about folks. I'm not going to keep you in suspense and I'm not going to play 'hard-to-get'. I know what you really want to hear and so here it is…"

The three disciples rose perfectly in time to a pitched crescendo,

"…yes I am the Messiah."

The crowd was stunned. A piece of bread fell from the open mouth of one of the Sadducees sat in the front row. A couple of people looked at each other, uncertain as to what the response to this bombshell should be. I milked the silence for a few moments before continuing.

"There, I said it. No messing around, no hiding the truth…I AM.

It's me, I'm Him, I'm the Christ. I'm your savior, I'm the One. I'm the one that's been prophesied about and I'm your only hope for salvation. Now that I've told you, none of you has an excuse. Listen to me and be saved."

I really wanted to make sure that I hadn't left any doubt in anyone's mind so I stepped forward, right to the edge of the mountain and shouted once more;

"Look, I just want to make absolutely, 100% sure that everyone is crystal clear about this. Has everybody got it? No mistakes? I'M THE CHRIST."

I clicked my fingers and the old man on the mat, lying strategically in front of the whole crowd suddenly jumped to his feet. I'd left him paralyzed for a few hours until I was ready to drop the grenade of being the Messiah and his suddenly leap had the effect I needed. The crowd screamed as one.

Once I was sure that it had sunk in, and once the murmurs had settled I carried on;

"Right then, now that that's out of the way I'm going to tell you a little story and then this little lad here has brought some fish sandwiches for everyone. Here we go then people, if you're sitting comfortably this is the story of the Prodigal Son;

There was a man who had two sons. The younger one said to his father, 'Father, give me my share of the estate.' So he divided his property between them.

Not long after that the younger son got together all he had, set off for a distant country and there squandered his wealth in wild living. After he had spent everything there was a severe famine in that whole country and he began to be in need. So he went and hired himself out to a citizen of that country who sent him to his fields to feed pigs. He longed to fill his stomach with the pods that the pigs were eating, but no one gave him anything.

When he came to his senses he said, 'How many of my father's hired men have food to spare and here I am starving to death! I will set out and go back to my father and say to him: Father, I have sinned against heaven and against you. I am no longer worthy to be called your son; make me like one of your hired men.' So he got up and went to his father.

But while he was still a long way off his father saw him and ran to the gate. Sliding the bolts across, he padlocked it. He also closed and locked the front door, drew the curtains shut and crouched beneath the window sill.

The son stood at the gates for a while knocking, but to no avail. He then started shouting, calling out to his father saying 'Father, I have sinned against heaven and against you. I am no longer worthy to be called your son'

"Flipping right you're not", his father yelled back, still hiding in the darkness "...you had your chance with me but chose to go off by yourself. You made your bed now go and sleep in it."

The son looked confused; "But Father I'm still your son. Plus...I don't have a bed! I've been sleeping with pigs!"

"I don't want to hear about your filthy city-ways, keep them to yourself. I've got nothing more for you here. I gave you your share, now you're on your own."

The father then had a bright idea. He whispered to his servants, 'Quick! Go and get my older son from the field where he's undoubtedly busy grafting. Bring the best robe you have and put it on him. Put a ring on his finger and sandals on his feet. Bring the fattened calf and kill it. Let's have a feast and celebrate. And make sure that the smell of it wafts over to that worthless son of mine by the gate." So they began to celebrate.

After a while the younger brother heard the music and dancing and smelled the cooking meat. So he called one of the servants near and asked him what was going on.

'Your brother has tirelessly worked day after day with your father while you've been off gallivanting around the country and so he's

decided to reward the one son that's actually worth anything with a feast. He's even killed the fattened calf to show how grateful he is for his dedication, loyalty and trust.'

Inside the party the father stood up to give a speech. Looking straight at the older brother and speaking loud enough to be heard all the way over by the gate, he said,

'All these years you've been slaving for me and have never disobeyed my orders. And yet I've never even given you a young goat so you could celebrate with your friends. I'm so sorry. Seeing this worthless wretch of a son come crawling home has made me realise what an amazing son you are and how grateful I should be. Have some fattened calf, on me.

The younger brother then went off, wept and gnashed his teeth a bit.

The End."

The crowd were silent, obviously blown away with the deep message I'd just laid out to them. I noticed a tear in someone's eye (although later I overheard that it could have been hay-fever) and saw that some of the children were so obviously shaken by the simplicity of the message that they couldn't even make eye contact with me, choosing instead to play loudly with each other on the floor.

After a few moments of silence, however I did start to hear some consternation. Some less-reputable members of the crowd were audibly heard mumbling things such as;

"Was that it?"

"So wait, am I supposed to be the younger brother, or the older one?"

"Is he still saying he's the Christ? Shouldn't we…you know…throw stuff at him?

"Where are the free biscuits I was promised?"

I realized that these poor souls were simply unable to grasp the deep, eternal truths of my parable and that therefore an explanation was needed. I know that some Rabbis leave people on cliff-hangers or don't fully explain their teaching, but that's not for me.

I need people saved and busy following me so why would I not spell out my message to them? Why should I make it hard for people to understand? An easy-to-comprehend, 3 point sermon explanation was required.

I quieted them down, and began;

"You see the deal is that, like I said earlier, I'm God..."

The already-frustrated crowd suddenly burst into uproar, only silenced when I zapped a man with an odd looking, disfigured ear and shrunk it back down to size. Pointing my finger slowly across the crowd, they all fell silent one by one. I tried to carry on;

"...so anyways, like I said I'm God. I'm the Father in that story. I made you; made the ground you're walking on and made everything you've ever had. And I've given it all to you. I've given you life, given you amazing gifts and talents, health, provisions and eternal love.

But, and here's my point number 1, SOME of you..." at the word "some", I leaned over and pointed into the crowd, terrified faces suddenly blushing and glancing hurriedly at their neighbors, "...have been acting like the younger brother. Going off and wasting the gifts I've given you. Doing your own thing, not listening to my Father and not staying close to me."

I gave them a moment to let it sink in before raising my voice and continuing;

"And so what do you deserve in return? Do you know how hard it is not to send another flood? Seriously I gave you people your

76

inheritance, gave you the prophets and gave you the whole history of your race and look what happened?! I predicted my coming, gave you the prophecies and am about to make your lives complete…"

The whole crowd was in the palm of my hand.

"…I made you lot, I blessed you and yet some of you DON'T EVEN BELIEVE I EXIST!! You moan about me when things go bad and then don't acknowledge me when things are good. You take all the good things I've given you and, like the younger brother you just go off and squander them and then come crawling back to me when you need something! When times get hard, when you suddenly realize how small, fragile and broken your lives are you suddenly come running back for another handout. Well things need to change, people!"

I paused for breath before continuing,

"Point number 2; do you know how many times a day I hear 'help me' or 'forgive me' by people who were not only saying the same thing yesterday but who'll be saying it tomorrow too? Do you know how many times I hear people asking for my blessing on their lives and who then just go off and abandon me?

What do you expect me to do when you come crawling back? Better still; ask yourselves what would you do? Would you just love and forgive someone who'd wronged you over and over and over again and who you knew would probably do the same again the very next day? Would you be able to love someone who'd cheated on you daily for their whole lives? Or would you love the one that's stuck by you, not left you or forsaken you? What would you do?

And lastly - point number 3 - put yourself in the older brother's shoes for one minute. Is it fair that God should just ignore the people who haven't run off? What should happen to the ones who've stuck by me, loved and obeyed me? These guys surely deserve the praise and love that's owed them otherwise what's the point of them staying so loyal? Why be my loyal disciple if I treat outcasts better than friends?"

I heard the murmur of understanding ripple through the crowd. I genuinely felt the conviction and guilt in their hearts as I drew it to a close.

"And so the point of this story is simple; if you're good, if you're like the older brother you'll be rewarded. You'll get what you've earned. If you're bad you'll get what you deserve too; you'll be locked out. If you want back in you're going to have to really come crawling on your knees. Don't get me wrong, I am still the God of second chances, but everyone has a limit. Grace can easily be exploited. And so if there's no consequences, why would anybody bother trying?"

I saw the nods and caught a glimpse of the shared smiles;

"And so I hope my message is clear to all of you out there; be like the older brother. Don't stray from me and don't be bad. Don't waste anything I've given you, don't go off on your own or else you're done-for. I've warned you enough over the years and I've certainly shown you the advantages of staying by my side. You know what'll happen so don't take this lightly. I am a God of justice – everyone gets what they deserve."

As the sermon finished and the boys quickly went round with the offering plate I looked out at the crowd, doing my best to portray the look of 'exhausted holy man'. I put on the wearying smile of someone from whom Gods immense power had obviously poured through. A couple of people smiled back but mostly they'd headed over to the food tables.

Peculiarly enough though, as the crowds dispersed it was the Pharisees who remained until the end. I could see them chatting amongst themselves, looking impressed and nodding to one another. Slowly they did eventually slink off but not before nodding in my direction. One of them even came over to shake my hand.

I guess it wasn't really the effect I was expecting, but it's nice that at least my message seems to have pleased someone. Tomorrow it's on to the Beatitudes (Blessed are the strong, blessed are the right, blessed are the generous etc). Hopefully it'll be another packed show and another full offering bag at the end also!

JR's Response

I'm warning you now that this is going to be a long response!

There's some good points in Matts version and a few very honest, human responses to what would seem like the very logical, practical way for God to do things. It also raises some questions that have been chatted about and discussed for ages;

Why wouldn't Jesus just come out and say exactly who He was?

Why wouldn't "the father" in the Prodigal son story make his wayward son prove that he really wanted to be back in the family and that he was truly repentant for his actions?

Why wouldn't Jesus just explain everything extremely clearly as opposed to all the mystery and the riddle-like-stories?

In response then, let's start out with the first question; why wouldn't Jesus just come out and let everyone know that He was the Messiah, that He was the Christ and that He'd come to save mankind from its utter destruction?

In Matthew 12 v 15-16 Jesus is recorded as doing something seemingly bizarre; He warns the crowd not to tell anyone who He was. As a self-promoter, Jesus sucked. Why would He do this?

To answer that I feel we must turn the initial question on its head; what would it mean to you for Jesus to be the Messiah? What would it mean to you for Him to be the Christ? What would it mean to you for Him to come back and save mankind from this utter destruction?

Depending on who I am asking those questions to will depend on what kind of response I will get. For example, I would get a different answer to that question depending on whether you were a faithful Jew, whether you were a Gentile, whether you were a Pharisee, a Levite, an Essene or one of the Sadducees.

Everyone and their dog had their opinions on what the Messiah would look like and be like when He returned. By no means was this something that everyone agreed on.

In the time of Jesus, in the midst of the Roman Empire in the first century the Jews would have seen the Messiah as a Davidic figure who was going to swoop into town, reclaim his rightful throne and restore power to Israel. He would be the "King of the Jews" and this oppressed nation of folks would finally rise up out of the shadows and take what they felt was rightfully theirs.

And honestly, after seeing some of the things that Jesus was capable of, would it really have been too far-fetched to believe that He also could have risen up and taken the throne? I mean the guy could make the lame walk, the deaf hear and gave sight to the blind. He could be in a boat in the middle of a tsunami and then calm the waves with just a few words. He could multiply a few fish and some bread to feed thousands. Would it have been such a stretch of the imagination to think that this same guy could have ruled the world?

Not at all.

But here's where the simple answer to the first question is revealed; it is for this very reason that He <u>did not</u> announce who He was. Had He done so, pandemonium would have broken out. The crowds would have made Him King by force. They would have displaced Herod, placed a crown of gold on His head, and waited expectantly for His first royal move - taking down Rome.

After all, a man who was capable of everything that Jesus was would make the worlds most powerful King, correct? And here's where we find the first problem. A man like Jesus could never be made a king on this earth. Why? Because He would immediately have been expected to step in and fix everything, for everyone. He would have been expected to have said yes to everyone, to have healed everybody, to have fed all the hungry, to have calmed every storm, to have made every grey sky sunny, to have turned every dingy cup of water into top-shelf wine, and to have "extreme-home-makeover-ed" this earth into a brand new Garden of Eden.

If Jesus was announced as the King at this point in history, heaven would have been expected on earth. But that time hadn't yet come; this was not the time or the place for Jesus to take his place on the throne.

The deal is (and this is as important today for us to realize as it was back then) that Jesus can't just say "yes" to everyone here on earth because of the effect it would have on our world.

In the movie "Bruce Almighty" the title character is complaining to God that he could do a lot better job if he had Gods powers and so God lets him try. He bestows all His powers unto him and pretty soon Bruce starts hearing everyone's prayers. It is so absolutely overwhelming that he decides to just answer everyone with a "yes", believing that in that way everyone will be happy.

Well, guess what happens? Absolute chaos. A "yes" to my prayer might very well be a "no" to your prayer and so then what happens? If two million people pray to win the lottery and they all do (thereby each only winning a tiny percentage of the prize) then how does that help anyone? It is a great movie with a very clear picture of why we're not God and why Jesus wasn't announcing himself as the new King – the responsibilities of that role weren't ready to be carried out yet.

This idea of God just answering "yes" to everyone leads into another simple reason why Jesus did not reveal to everyone who He was. Jesus was not a genie or a biblical Santa Claus. He was not on earth so people could just come up to Him, make a wish and go about their day. He was not here to perform and to be a side-show attraction. In some respects He did everything He could to downplay His miraculous events and to slip under the public radar.

However, if He were to reveal to the world who He really was, then a Miracle-Maker He would become. In the gospels, after Jesus heals people He often tells them not to tell anyone what just happened. Why? Because He doesn't want people to see Him merely as a traveling miracle-worker who puts on shows from time to time. The miracles themselves are only catalysts of something else; salvation. Sins are forgiven after paralysis is healed. Adulterers are protected but only before being instructed on how to live their new lives. Jesus' miracles are never the be-all-and-end-all of His mission they are only there to either prove His power, to serve as an example of His word or as a precursor to His true purpose; the salvation of sinners. He was not a magician. He was not a showman. He was not someone you went to so that if you were lucky you might get your wishes granted like the guy down the street did.

The reality was that if Jesus had come forward and said that He was the Messiah people would have immediately started thinking He was a genie in a bottle. Would it then have really been that difficult for Him to get followers?

Who wouldn't want to follow that guy? Despite Jesus' efforts at dissuading the crowd from telling who He was, despite His best attempts at keeping a low profile He was already swamped by followers, desperate to see a miracle. Look at John 6 v 26. Jesus explains clearly that the people aren't there to hear His words or even to see people healed, they're merely following Him for a free lunch.

If Jesus had said He was the Messiah people would have followed Him because of what they could have got from Him. He fed 5000 at a sitting and this would have become a regular expectation.

I've always wondered; if I were a rich and famous sports star like I said I'd always wished to be, how would I ever know who my real friends were? How would I know if some girl I met really liked me for me or if she just liked me because I was famous and I had lots of money? How would I ever know if the folks following me really believed in me or if they were just along for the ride because of what I had and what they might get out of the deal? Would all of those people still love me and want to be around me if I was just a regular guy? How would I ever know?

I don't know if you could ever know.

By not revealing who Jesus really was and by keeping all the miracles and supernatural things as quiet as He could then it allowed him to have a real good idea that the folks following Him were following Him not just for a free lunch, but because they really did believe in Him. They weren't along just for the ride or just for what He could do to satisfy the hunger in their bellies, but for what He could do to satisfy their souls. By keeping it quiet it weeded out the pretenders. And here's an essential point about our Christian faith;

In the Old testament God shows up as a pillar of fire and a pillar of smoke. He sweeps the entire oceans aside at a glance, pulling them back to destroy the Egyptian armies. He sends plagues, He sends manna, He sends visions and He performs miracles. He does everything He can to make Himself as visible and as obvious as possible to the Israelites. And at the end of all that, what kind of faith do these people have?

The second that Gods back is turned they fall away. They build idols. They whinge. They whine. They worry. They disobey. They abandon.

I often hear this phrase;

"If God would only <u>show me</u> He existed, I'd believe…"
I always want to answer "Really? Because that didn't work out too well for the Israelites." The moment the miracles stopped, so did their faith.

I often wonder if Jesus kept a low profile so that people weren't believing in the miracle, rather than the man. I often wonder if the reason He is mysterious about His mission, the reason He downplays the miracles and the reason He hides the true fact about His role is that He knows that true faith comes from believing-without-always-seeing. That if people couldn't see He was the Messiah for themselves they were blinded to the truth and merely following for a free lunch.

True faith comes when you believe, even when God isn't performing miracles. A Jewish refugee wrote on his German cell wall in World War II;

"I believe in the sun, even when it's not shining. I believe in love, even when I don't feel it. And I believe in God, even when He is silent"

Perhaps, by Jesus intentionally hiding his true calling as the Messiah, those that still followed Him, those that activated their brains and could see the truth of who He really was, those people were counted by Him as His true followers.

It's this same thought process which leads into one of the other points made previously in this chapter.

Why didn't Jesus just explain all the stories, nice and simply, to everyone around?

Why the need for all the mystery?

Well, in very similar fashion to the last point, Jesus wanted to know who really wanted to know what He was all about. By talking in parables and telling all these creative stories He found out whose hearts were genuinely seeking the will of God and who were just caught up in the scene.

Why do we like television shows like Twin Peaks or Lost? Because they make us activate our brains and chase after the truth. They don't spoon feed us the storylines, we have to work out what's going on.

It's the same reason that, for generations, we have loved mystery novels, detective stories and surprise endings – the pay-off is in working out what's really happening rather than have the author spelling it out for you.

With Jesus, He knew that the folks who really wanted to know the will of God, the folks who really wanted to pursue Jesus and follow Him, the folks who really wanted to humble themselves and learn from this Rabbi would question Him. They would follow up Jesus' parables and try to figure out what the heck these stories meant. They would ask questions. They would come to dinner and chat with Him. They would seek out truth. These weren't the free-lunch hopers. These were the true believers.

What is really sad is that we currently live in a world where we think we want all the answers spelled out for us. We take out our phones and ask the internet before we even think about an answer ourselves. Information is suddenly accessible to everyone - which is amazing and important - but it does come at a price. Faith comes from seeking. If we want someone to just serve us our faith on a silver platter with as little effort on our part as possible we wont ever be true followers of Christ.

The saddest part is that church and the preachers of the world seem to cater to this mentality and I am as guilty as anyone. We preach sermons that spell out everything for the listener. We give them a sweet little poem and a PowerPoint. The message gives them every Scripture to go to with every point. It puts all these points into a nice little 1,2,3 formula and we tell stories to illustrate our points, then makings sure we've explained the story precisely so that no one is confused at the end of the sermon. We make sure that the listener has everything they need to get through however many days until the next message.

There is nothing wrong with making the gospel easy-to-understand, please don't think I'm saying that. But there is also something to be said for mystery. For leg-work. For digging yourself. As the old saying goes;

"The man who chops the wood, warms himself twice."

The act of finding out the truth is, in itself as much of a blessing and an act of faith as understanding it. If we forget that Jesus sometimes plays "hard-to-get" so that people will, themselves, have to chase after Him we miss half of the effect of faith.

If a sermon listener has zero work to do on their own, where is the act of faith on their behalf? Where is the learning? Where is the growing? They don't have to go home and dig into Scripture and find out what the heck I was talking about. They don't have to sit around with their friends and try and figure out what that story was about. They don't really have to do much of anything except show up.

If we feed people, but don't encourage them to exercise what do we end up with? Fat, lazy listeners.

Also to top it off we end up sugar-coating the message and avoid chatting about the difficulties and struggles that come along with following Christ. And here's the real truth; Jesus needs to be followed. We cant do that by sitting down. Effort is needed.

Jesus sometimes makes it difficult for people to understand the real message without getting up and following Him. He almost seems to place obstacles in their path (mountains, lakes, hunger, vagueness) and make His words tough to grasp. Why? Because those people that have committed themselves to navigating the obstacles, committed themselves to finding out the truth, those people that have invested effort are the people He wants.

Lost had me gripped for 6 seasons. By season 3, I was already that invested in it that I knew nothing would stop me from reaching the end. I had to find out answers, I had already come too far to stop.

Jesus' parable messages weren't difficult to understand. They didn't need a cryptic-key, or vast intelligence from the listener to be able to understand. But they did need interpreting. He was willing to give answers – <u>but only to those who were willing to ask Him.</u>

In a world that is defined by numbers and one that is charted and graphed, graded and accounted by financial gains and losses the church has gotten caught up in this and has become scared of the truth and scared to encourage some of the mystery. I sometimes wonder if we want to make sure that nobody has room to breathe and a have a thought of their own because if they do that, then we just might lose them.

Well why are we afraid of losing these people?

If we point out how truly hard being a disciple of Christ can be then yes, they might not come back next week. If we don't tell them exactly what that story meant then yes, they might not understand it.

But Jesus didn't seem to care about either of these.

This might be one of the areas where the church has strayed from the message of Jesus more than anything.

Jesus knew that He would lose people from the get-go. Whole crowds walked away and abandoned Him. He knew that there would be disciples who started following Him but then found it too hard and fell to the side. He knew that people would be confused by His stories and yet He kept telling them. He knew that folks wouldn't like what He had to say, but He kept saying it.

Matt told me this story once;

"I saw an insurance salesman in the mall yesterday, standing, looking desperate in the middle of the lobby, clipboard in hand. Immediately I took out my phone and pretended to be talking, crossing in front of him and pointing at my phone when he leered

closer. On my way back I did the same. In total I think I must have crossed in front of that guy about 4 times, each time making my excuses when he tried to talk to me.

Today we've been doing an evacuation drill at work. Two firefighters, dressed in Breathing Apparatus were searching for a body inside our smoke-house when those of us outside mimicked an evacuation signal; short, sharp bursts on a whistle. When the firefighters hear that simple signal they know that the building is about to collapse (something we can only see from the outside) and they evacuate."

Matt and I both drew the same conclusion about these two occurrences; too often we Christians act like the insurance salesman rather than as the whistle blower.

Too often we appear like desperate salesmen, eager to earn our commission by making appealing deals to people in our sermons or our ministry. We are terrified of offending people or of them not fully understanding the truth and leaving us. We chase people down, we beg and coerce and we act as if we need to sell the gospel to them.

When in fact we should be whistle-blowers. Jesus was. Jesus knew the truth; that these peoples lives were collapsing around them and that only he had the simple short, sharp message that could save them. We need to act as the people outside the burning building, seeing it collapsing and blowing the whistle. If people hear the message, if they evacuate then they can be saved. If they choose to ignore it, at least we have given them warning.

Jesus never chased after people who left. He never acted like the salesman, trying to sell them something or desperate for commission. He told people the truth and if they chose to ignore it, chose to leave, so be it.

We seem desperate to make things as elementary as possible because we are desperate for people to fill our sanctuaries. Jesus seemed perfectly fine with things being fairly hard to grasp and if that meant losing folks, then that was the way it had to be.

He wanted to know, without a shadow of a doubt that those folks choosing to follow Him were for real and that they would follow Him to the ends of the earth and eventually to their death in a lot of cases.

Why don't we live in a world where we demand this type of discipleship? Look at how appealing mystery is! Yes, we have a lot of couch-potatoes in the world but we also have people filling our gyms! Some people will want to follow God even if we're honest with them about how hard it is. We have people who thrive on effort, who want a mission to struggle at and who want a way of life that takes a bit of leg-work. Why aren't we appealing to those people?!

Perhaps if we're honest we just want rear-ends in the pews or money in our budget, and if this means our churches are filled with watered-down believers then that is an allowance that we've been willing to make.

God knew exactly what He was doing by not having Jesus reveal to the world who He was at that time and He knew what He was doing by speaking in parables. Weeding out true believers.

If we've ascertained anything from this book so far then one thing has to be a loud and resounding truth; God does not do things and Jesus did not do things how we would do them. Finally we see that all the more clearly in the original "Prodigal Son" story.

So much has already been written about this parable and in the spirit of what has already been said I encourage you to go and do some digging! Go and read about it!

All I want to focus on, to finish this chapter is one particular difference in the way Jesus told the story. It is in this parable that one of the most beautiful pictures of God's love is revealed and at the same time it is also one of the most powerful truths of Scripture.

In the version you read before the first half of the story is a spot on, word-for-word translation. You have a kid who thinks he knows best and that there is more for him out there in the big ol' world, so he asks his father for his share of the inheritance and he leaves. He goes about from place to place just living it up. He's going to the hottest clubs, eating in the finest restaurants, buying the nicest cars, wearing the swankiest clothes, hooking up with various women and just partying like a rock star.

Before too long, as you might guess, he runs out of money. His partying days over, his friends all gone and there - hungry and homeless - he laments to himself. He ends up taking a job as a servant, feeding pigs and he longs to eat as well as the pigs were doing.

It was in this time of desperation that he realized that even his father's servants lived a luxurious life compared to this, so he decided to dive into that humble pie and head home.

Here is where Scripture and Matts version begin to differ.

The version above, as expected gives a very human response to the prodigal son's return. He was not welcomed. His father had been betrayed. Hurt. Embarrassed and humiliated. He was not accepted with open arms and he was not looked at fondly by his father. Even after the father eventually lets him back in the house he makes it very clear that it would take a lot of effort and a lot of time to earn back his father's love, respect and trust and to become part of the family once again.

There was no way that the son was going to take his inheritance, walk out the door, turn his back on everything that had been done for him, waste away everything he'd been given and then when times were tough be able to just stroll back home like nothing had ever happened...not in this house.

And just to prove this to the ungrateful son the father brings in the other son from the fields and tells him that he is going to throw him a party and thank him for being such a wonderful, devout son. He even goes to the extreme of making sure that the food they're grilling can be smelt from just outside the fence just so that the ungrateful brother can smell it and experience the hurt the father was stung with.

Fortunately for you and me the God of the Bible is not like the father in this story. I don't want to focus on the son in this instance but instead to look at the father.

In the real story, the one in Scripture, the father sees his son from a long way off and he runs to him. He drops everything and busts out into a dead sprint all the way out to the road to wrap his arms around his boy who has finally come home. I'll be honest in saying that I get choked up just about every time I read this story.

The father comes out to the son. Mercy comes to the undeserving, forgiveness to the lost and love to the unlovely.

The father's grace is so much greater and bigger than anything we might be able to wrap our minds around without being parents ourselves, and even then it proves so hard to justify. This fathers love for his son knows no bounds. All he cares about is the fact that he is home.

He not only welcomes him in the door but is so excited for his son to be home that he throws him a party. He brings him a fancy robe and some swanky jewelry to put on. He brings in the fatted calf and the best booze and they just party into the night.

Imagine for a minute where the father in Jesus' version is coming from. He didn't know if his son was dead or alive. He didn't know where on earth he was. In fact he didn't know if he'd ever see him again. How many nights do you think this father wept just lying in bed imagining the worse? How many times do you think he sat there, filled with regret, at what could have been?

Then years later he sees his beloved son come walking down the street.

What did Jesus' version of the father feel right then? Anger? Disbelief? Revenge? No. His heart must have literally broke in pieces seeing his son at a distance and he couldn't do anything but run to him, wrap his arms around him and hold him.

What kind of father is this? Doesn't he want the boy to learn his lesson? Doesn't he feel that he deserves answers, apologies, begging regret and crawling repentance? Where is the justice? Where is the boys changed heart; he's come back because he's run out of money not because he realized he was at fault. Why does the father act in such an embarrassing, self-deprecating, pride-less and humiliating manner?!

Because simply, Gods love for you is a reckless, dangerous, vulnerable and unconditional love that breaks all the rules.

This is the God of the Bible and this is the father that I follow. This is a God of 2nd, 3rd, 4th, 5th, 6th, and 592nd chances. It is a love that we can never comprehend and a grace that we will never deserve. It is an adoration for His creation and for His children that we will never be able to make sense of, no matter what we do.

I cannot fathom this father. Like Matt, if I was the father I'd have wanted answers, wanted to see repentance and wanted to see regret.

But I'm not the father. I'm the son. And despite the fact that I wouldn't have believed it possible, that's the kind of father I would desperately want. The fathers response is the best I could have imagined it, if I was returning home. It'd have been beyond my wildest dreams. I'd have been expecting the pig-house and received rings, expected to have had to make a lengthy apology and received a bear-hug, expected to have had to grovel and instead have received overwhelming forgiveness without ever having to say a word.

This father, this God is one that says, "I don't care where you've been and how royally you've messed up. All I want to do is see you walking back home to me so I can sprint out to the street and wrap my arms around you and hold you."

It is a God that says "Have you seen some of the characters I've used throughout the Bible?! Murderers, adulterers, traitors, cowards…and you don't think I can deal with the things you've done? Come on home. I love you."

It is a God that never gives up on us and longs for nobody to perish.

It is a God that throws the checklists away and says we can start over.

It is a God that will never turn His back on us, no matter what.

Matt's version doesn't change the actions of the son, it alters the actions of the father. It's an acknowledgment that if we were God, we wouldn't be able to cope with humanities sinfulness, their lack of repentance and their overwhelming abandonment of their creator.

But God is more than us. Our father is a God that loves us so much that He knew more often than not that we'd be exactly like the prodigal son in the story. So He sent His one and only son to die on the cross so that we'd forever have a second chance. So that forever we would have hope. So that at the end of it all we could all walk home, ashamed at all the mistakes we'd made and He could run out to us all and wrap His gigantic, eternally loving arms around us and hold us forever.

That is the father we follow.

Chapter Five
Sending Out the Disciples

Well, this sucks. John's been put in prison. This is bad, no two ways about it. I love that guy. I had planned on breaking him out, on sending an army of angels to politely knock on the jail door (after all, it's the least he deserves, right?) but I got waylaid. Oddly though, before I could do anything to help he sent his disciples to me to ask me if I was the Christ. Bit confusing really as I thought we had this thing in the bag already. The conversation went as follows;

"Are you the one to come, or should we expect someone else?"

I wasn't sure at first how to answer;

"Um…are you kidding me? I just brought that guy over there back from the dead. I mean seriously, are you mental? Of course I'm the Christ!"

They seemed happy with that and went on their way, and that was that. Still it put me in an odd frame of mind – how could John question me like that? My mood recently hasn't been helped by the disciples constant bickering. Only yesterday I caught them trying to work out who would be the greatest in the kingdom of heaven. When I told them, simply that it would be Peter it did shut them up for a bit. Well, except for Peter who now won't stop harping on about it. Maybe I need to rethink that decision.

To be honest these guys are driving me insane. I honestly cannot remember how many times I've made them write down "I must not freak out when Jesus dies as He'll be back 3 days later" on the lapel of their tunic. Even despite this, even despite my near constant reminders they still don't seem to get it. They don't seem to get any of it in fact. Finally I even gave in and told them that I'd be coming back for good on October 9th, 2034 just so they'd stop going on about it.

Mainly due to their whining and incessant questioning, I've decided to send them out. I need to reach the target demographics near Samaria anyways and I can't do that solely with the tour dates I have booked in Jerusalem. So I'm sending them off on their own and giving them their own little missions to carry out. Before they leave, however I'm giving them a little pep-talk. This is what I have so far;

"The harvest is plentiful but the workers are few. I am trusting all this to you 3 as you're the only ones remotely qualified for the role. You guys are going to have to work blooming hard to reap in this whole crop. Be aggressive, be assertive, this is our one shot. Go door to door and don't be afraid to give the hard-sell. Don't take no for an answer. I'm sending you out as wolves amongst...other wolves, I guess.

The pressure's on you guys, the spotlight is shining. You're my voice and my mouthpieces so don't screw this up. Whatever you look like, I'll look like. However you act will reflect on me. Rule number one - don't make me look bad. People are going to base their choice of accepting salvation on what your "church" ends up looking like. That all starts with you. I picked you because you're inscrutable so don't let me down.

With that in mind, wear a suit. Shirt and tie at least. And Andrew, for heaven's sake (literally) sort your hair out. No one trusts a man with a dirty beard.

When you enter a town set up shop with the most important family you can. Find the Mayor if possible or at least a family that has connections. Try and organize a rally/healing event/speaking arrangement and, whatever you do don't be a burden to people. They shouldn't have to pay for your upkeep and so yesterday I made some denarii appear from some fishes mouths. You shouldn't need more financial support than these fishy coins."

As well as the cash I've prepared their provisions too; boxes of scrolls, posters, indoor pyrotechnics, lighting rigs, sound systems, prayer boxes, collection plates and mini-donuts that they'll need for their events. I guess they're going to need bigger donkeys.

When it comes to what they're actually going to talk to people about, I've decided to be extra-specially prescriptive about it. Later on down the line I've got a feeling that certain things are going to prove to be real "bees-in-bonnets" to some people. It only makes sense then that I cover all the points now so that there's no confusion. People are going to want to know what my priorities are and what I really care about. These then are the bullet points of what I want the disciples to discuss when I send them out;

1. The role of church and state, praying to the saints, and whether or not confession and a priest is needed. Let's just say that I reckon it'll be easier all around in the future if I'm especially clear what I want people to do in this respect.

2. Homosexuality. This is obviously a major bug-bear of mine (I do talk about it frequently) and is going to be a major topic in the future so I need it covered in full.

The same goes for;

3. Women in the ministry

4. Alcohol, swearing and church dress-code

5. Predestination (an utter minefield)

After that I want the guys to move on to discuss;

6. What type of worship music I like and will allow. Exactly how loud is "too-loud", the balance between new and old hymns, how many repeated chorus' symbolize "spiritual guidance" and whether or not drums are a good thing.

7. Speaking in tongues. I've actually written out an exact phonetic description of what I'll allow tongues to sound like in my services, so there won't be any "experimentation".

When and only when these points have been laid out and my opinion on them has been fully explained, the disciples may then move on to these;

8. Baptism. What age, how, where and what format.

9. The role of the candle in the church. This may also include discussion on incense, color schemes, church seating arrangements (to pew or not to pew) and how to carry out communion (in chairs, with little glasses, or up the front)

10. What time in the morning a service should begin and how long a sermon should last for.

11. A.O.B.

(During this "Any Other Business" section the disciples may field questions on minor issues; whether grape-juice is a sufficient compromise to wine, how tall a church steeple should be, dog collars, when to raise hands during singing, how to pray, what to do with our enemies, grace, forgiveness, how to please God and how to be saved etc.)

I know it might seem anal but I just feel that it's important for people to get a grip of what my mission is all about. I want clarity, I want no wiggle-room. I have a huge amount to say on all of these topics and the last thing I want is division and confusion as my church begins to grow.

It's much better if I just lay it all out on the line now so that there's no mistake for future generations of believers. Yes it's important that they learn about how I'm going to save them but surely the gospels that are going to be written about me will be big enough to also include some simple descriptions regarding how much I want my followers to give, whether children should stay in the main services and whether or not short-haired women should be allowed to hear my word at all.

Prescription is the order of the day. It's why I'm entrusting my message to just these three disciples; I want people to know exactly what I think and precisely how I want to be followed. Disorder, chaos and messiness aren't me. I want a unified church all singing off the same hymn sheet. Seriously, I want one single hymn sheet with my top ten hits on it, and that's the lot. No worries then about style or bias, about interpretation or individual leanings. Exactness equals evangelical excellence.

I hate to admit it but all this talk about leaving a legacy has meant that I'm also starting to look to the future. Every time I see a tree I shudder. I know what's coming and I'll be honest in saying that I've spent most nights this week praying for another way out of this. The truth is that I don't want to die. I have to find another way before it's too later. I don't want to go out like that.

JR's Response

Does anybody out there like riddles?

Or solving a mystery?

Or having all the pieces to the puzzle and just trying to figure out how to put it together?

Or for you math nerds out there like me, trying to solve a proof?

I love these kinds of things. I love someone giving me the basic info that I need and then having to use that to figure out the bigger picture. I love trying to solve the mystery. Like we touched on last time there is just something about having to figure it out that makes the final result that much more appealing. If someone just spells it out for me and hands me the finished product it is just not as rewarding.

As we've already seen, Jesus does this a lot.

He wants us to figure things out. I imagine he delights in seeing us find the solutions.

Now Jesus could very easily have spelled everything out, under the sun for us to do. He could have given us the manual on "How to live life as a follower of Christ" or written the oh-so-popular best-seller "Christianity for Dummies" but He didn't.

Jesus relished the working-out part.

He spoke in parables and gave people riddle-like stories to figure out. He quoted the Old Testament and then let those words just hang, needing the listener to go and dig for recognition of their meaning. And much of the time He just didn't say anything at all. This, above all else would've frustrated the heck out of me.

Before we get started on this though, let me just quickly address the section dealing with John. Right away in this chapter we see Him upset about John's imprisonment, which would have been a perfectly natural response for Jesus. These guys were close, they were blood, they had a heart for this lost world and now John was sitting in prison.

I personally have always wondered why there was never a plan to bust him out of the slammer. Jesus could have done so in a heartbeat being God and all! The truth is - and this is hard teaching to accept - as much as Jesus would have wanted to organize a heavenly escape attempt that just wasn't part of the plan. You can imagine how badly it must have hurt Jesus to know that He could've done something but then not been able to. Or allowed to.

This, sadly is an important lesson for us all. Sometimes tragedy strikes, sometimes horrible things happen, sometimes we get injured, we get hurt or we lose people we love and the truth of the matter is that if we mean what we say about the power and might of God then every single time He could have done something about it, but He doesn't. He just seems silent. He just seems to be doing lots of other things and saying lots of other things except the one thing we long to hear; that He will step in and save the day.

I'm sure that John would not have minded if Jesus had stepped in to save the day for him while he was in prison. So why was this not the case?

In Luke 7 (amongst other chapters) John sends his disciples to Jesus to ask Him if He is the Messiah or not. In the gospels Jesus responds in riddle-like fashion, quoting various passages in Isaiah, where it talks about the one who is to come and the deliverance that will take place.

In these various passages (Isaiah 26:19; 29:18-19; 35:5-6; 61:1) it talks about all kinds of different signs and miracles that will be seen. These passages mention the dead being raised, the deaf hearing, the blind seeing, the lame walking, the mute speaking, lepers cured, good news being preached to the poor and freedom for the captives locked up in prison.

Now (and here is where Jesus becomes a master of coded language) as He is quoting all of these passages and listing out all of these things that are mentioned in relation to this so-called deliverance, He brings up just about everything listed above, except one, rather large and important thing.

If you look at what Jesus says in Luke 7:21-23 and then you compare it to all the things it talks about in Isaiah you should see one glaring difference.

Now you and I would probably not notice anything as we are reading through chapter 7 of Luke. We would not think twice about the list of things that Jesus tells John's disciples to go and report on but that's because we're no experts on the Old Testament.

But as Jewish disciples of a Jewish Rabbi, John's disciples would have known the Old Testament like the back of their hand. They would know it like we know songs on the radio or poems we memorize in grade school. They would have known every in and out of the Old Testament, so much so that if you were to start quoting certain things and you missed a spot they would catch on to it immediately.

And this is why, as his disciples repeated Jesus' words verbatim, John would have been listening to the things that Jesus had rattled off and his heart would have just crumbled.

Let me explain...

As Jesus mentioned the blind receiving sight and the lame walking it would have triggered a memory of a particular passage. As He mentions the deaf hearing and the lepers being healed it would have brought a different passage to mind. As He mentioned the dead being raised it would have reminded them of another. And when He mentioned the preaching of the good news to the poor it would have chimed in a last memory, which would have been especially interesting to John and his circumstances.

The passage about the preaching the good news to the poor comes out of Isaiah 61:1 and it mentions preaching good news to the poor and then it is followed in the same verse by a bit about proclaiming freedom for the captives and the release of prisoners.

Do you think this might have been relevant to John right then and there? As a captive in prison, do you think his heart might have been racing in expectation of Jesus' next words?

But if we look at the passage in Luke and at what Jesus tells John's disciples to report back, what does Jesus leave off?

The bit about releasing the captives...

I'm sure John was like "Wait a second!! Are you guys sure He didn't say anything else? Are you sure you're not just missing something? What about the bit about freeing the captives, release from prison? What about that?"

How heart-breaking would that have been?!?

104

Unfortunately (and again, this is hard teaching) sometimes Jesus is silent. And sometimes this silence hurts. Freedom, for John, wasn't part of the plan. It's not easy to say, harder to read and nearly impossible to understand, but it's universally true. The Sovereignty of God sometimes sucks.

However, and here's where I want to draw the main section of my response from, most of the time His silence says so much more than we can imagine. I only have 3 things to say about this;

First off we see that when the disciples are arguing about who is greater or wondering about who is greatest in the kingdom of Heaven, Jesus says things like, the last will be first and the least will be greatest.

It's clear then that sometimes he can make things specifically clear...

We also see that when Jesus is asked about the "end of the age" He says that no one knows, not even the angels or the Son.

And so sometimes He can seem pretty silent...

It just doesn't appear like Jesus is too concerned about nailing some things down. We see this same sort of vague direction when He sends out the disciples;

He says in Matthew 10 that they are to go and preach that "the kingdom of heaven is near" and in Luke 10 He tells them to say, "the kingdom of God is near you" which obviously are just about as clear as you can be, right?!

Clear as mud. What is He actually asking them to say? Would you not, as a disciple want a bit more training and input before being sent out?!

Preaching that the kingdom of Heaven is near can mean a ton of different things to a ton of different people. I bet that if you took a poll of a 100 people as to what they thought that meant that you'd get 100 different answers.

But there it is in scripture; Jesus gives them some very basic instructions and sends them on there way. In fact most of the instructions they do receive have to do with helping people (healing, cleansing and such) and not about preaching at them. It certainly doesn't include instructions regarding specific fine-print issues in the fledgling churches constitution.

Jesus wants them to be men of action and not men of many words, it seems. As it says in 1 John 3, "let us not love with <u>words</u> or tongue but with <u>actions</u> and in truth." Jesus' silence was an echo of what he expected of them; they were to be apostles who spoke loudest through their actions. They weren't men with all the answers, ready to batter down every argument with a well rehearsed response, but men willing to get their hands dirty.

Not only does He not give them specific instructions but He doesn't even allow them to take a lot of provisions with them. He seems to want them to walk by faith; in how they respond to folks, how they handle different crowds, how they interpret His message and how they physically live out there mission. His silence in preparing them isn't due to arrogance, ignorance or apathy; He knows that the Spirit will fill in the blank spaces and that Gods voice is the only one needed to speak in the silence.

Now let me go ahead and clear something up real quick for all those who are getting a little nervous out there; I'm not saying that we should all be silent! I'm not saying that preparation isn't important. I'm also especially not saying that I don't think that Jesus hasn't given us specific missions or that "all roads lead to God" or anything like that. What I do mean is that He has given us some freedom in how we do things. We, with the Spirits guidance, can fill in the gaps sometimes. He didn't leave us a check sheet for how to do mission or a ten-point guide on how to run a church service. His silence on these matters speaks volumes.

Let's cut to the chase; Jesus doesn't ever talk about many of the things that the church today seems to spend a lot of time talking about (and when I say "talking about" I really mean arguing and fighting about for centuries).

We Christians will happily split up a church over the color of the carpet, the font in the bulletin or the choice of playing a guitar over an organ. We take the freedom that Christ has given us in mission and somehow feel that everyone should fill in the blanks the same way. We somehow take the fact that Jesus was silent about certain things as a cue for us to shout our own interpretation as the only-way, forgetting that the silence can be filled in other ways too.

Remember – Jesus is crystal-clear about certain things but murkily silent about others. Some things obviously needed setting in stone whereas others were left in blank spaces.

If we'd take the silence of Jesus as serious as we take the words of Jesus then we'd learn a whole lot about Gods priorities and our own role in this messy, wonderful ministry.

Truly if we'd take the silences of Jesus as serious as we take some little verse at the end of 1 Corinthians 14 or at the beginning of Ephesians then we might just all be better off. Do we forget about the times that Jesus is quiet, perhaps assuming that He forgot to spell out certain aspects of the faith? What if He didn't forget? What if those things are left up to us to explore?

What if the music we use in church is up to us? With not one "better" than the other just a different method of worshipping? What if pre-destination isn't as cut-and-paste as we make out?

The truth is that if I was God (and that's a whole other book!), this is exactly how I'd want it to be. What kind of father restricts his children from making any decisions at all in their lives? Tells them what to wear, how to act, how to play, how long to play, who to make friends with, who to ignore, when to be home, when to sleep, what to dream about and most importantly <u>how to love them</u>?

Yes, fathers need to be crystal clear about certain things in order to make sure their children grow up correctly. But in other things, the joy of being a parent is in seeing the creativity, the imagination, the interpretation and the cultivation of the love and effort you've put into that child come through in their own expressions.

At the time of writing Matt's just had a son, Noah. I know for a fact that he's going to be honest with Noah about some things he should do and some things he shouldn't do as that boy grows up. But I know that Matt's not going to force Noah to become a fireman or to prescribe exactly what fathers day presents he should receive or to channel him down a single path of only choosing mountain-biking as a hobby. I know that Matt's excited to see how Noah turns out. I imagine God feels the same about us.

The truth is that God is big enough to be worshipped in many different ways and that's clear from the blank spaces he leaves. I'm not being Unitarian – there are some things that Jesus is completely clear about that are unshakeable. But there are others that can be interpreted differently and I believe that God relishes creativity.

Perhaps the problem lies with the value we put on what Jesus says, and on what He doesn't say. I sometimes wonder if we share Jesus' priorities, and this is my second point;

Jesus was cornered at one point in His ministry and was asked, straight up what <u>the most important thing</u> was for us to do. I mean, this was going to be <u>his greatest commandment</u>, and He could have said just about anything;

He could have said that evangelism was the end all be all of life here on earth.

He could have defined the roles of women in ministry.

He could have talked about alcohol or dancing.

He could have mentioned predestination and how He was simply the contemporary to the teachings of John Calvin.

He could have talked about the Holy Spirit and speaking in tongues.

He could have talked about anything at all, and yet in the end He talked about <u>one</u> thing.

He said that loving God and loving each other was the <u>greatest commandment</u>. These were His priorities. And it's not just Him that says it;

Romans 13:9 says, "The commandments, "Do not commit adultery," "Do not murder," "Do not steal," "Do not covet," and whatever other commandment there may be, are summed up in this one rule: "Love your neighbor as yourself", and Galatians 5:14 says, "The entire law is summed up in a single command: "Love your neighbor as yourself."

These seem pretty clear. Everything is summed up in one rule: love your neighbor as yourself. The entire law is summed up in a single command: love your neighbor as yourself. I just had to repeat it to point out the clarity. Jesus makes very clear the things that really matter to Him and then stays silent about others.

So my question is why on earth do we spend so much energy, emotion, tears and frustration arguing and drawing lines in the sand about things all over the place that are not spelled out half as clearly as this? Why, sometimes, do we spend <u>too much</u> time trying to decipher the blank spaces and not long enough looking at the blindingly obvious?!

Instead, why don't we just focus on the places where Jesus speaks loud and clear?

As a pastor, if I am completely honest I feel that the church has created a more rigid structure of rules and regulations than Jesus ever did. I know of plenty of churches out there who, if Jesus were to show up at their doors today would prevent Him from becoming a deacon because of certain aspects of His life that they would not approve of.

I know of a few churches that wouldn't hire Jesus to be on staff because of the fact that He was a single male.

Heck, there's a church right down the street that wouldn't even let Jesus be on leadership because He likes to go to dinner and have a drink with His friends.

Does that seem weird to anyone else? That Jesus, the only perfect man to ever live, the Messiah, God in human form wouldn't even be allowed to teach Sunday school in some of our churches??

I can't help but giggle at that one.

Jesus believed in us and had faith in us. He gave us some very important commands to get the ball rolling and then He shut up sometimes. He gave us freedom sometimes. He left it up to us sometimes.

And really, primarily we should be routing ourselves with Jesus' priorities rather than worrying about the peripherals.

How do you describe your church to others?

"They have a band", "They do communion sitting down", "They read liturgy", "They have a woman preacher", "They're traditional (hilarious really, when you think about the meaning of that word...see Acts if you don't understand)", "They're 'high church'"

When do you hear the phrase "My church? Well my church says we should love God and love each other." I'd argue not regularly. So where are our priorities lying?

If you're a Baptist, fantastic. Get those heads wet all you like but never forget your primary priority is loving God and loving each other. If you're a Methodist, go to town on that method but don't forget that your primary priority is loving God and loving each other. If you're C of E, you read those prayers out, if you're evangelical put your hands in the air, if you're Pentecostal, stick some ear plugs in and belt out those tunes but all of you don't forget that your primary priority is to love God and to love each other.

We should be known as Christians. We should be known for what we have in common, not our peripheral differences. When I reach heaven will Jesus look me over for my particular denomination or worship style? No, He'll look to see if Christ has me covered.

And here's my last point;

None of Jesus' silences were accidental. We were in mind the whole time.

He knew that my generation would need different things to reach them than my grandparents did. He knew that technology would add an element to worship that they didn't have to deal with at other points in history. He knew that our individual gifts would play themselves out in all kinds of different ways that would cause ministry to take on new shapes and styles.

And that's ok! Jesus came to save us, and made the gospel simple enough for anyone to believe in, regardless of their diversity.

If we really believe that the word of God is living and active then we will allow for it to lead us in different ways, at different times and in different scenarios. God is bigger than our rules, our thoughts, our prejudices, our preconceived notions and our biased expectations of what church should look like.

I am not, again, saying that there aren't unshakeable truths. There are. But there are also a vast array of peripheral things, some of which will never make sense until we reach heaven itself. The issue comes when, by emphasizing these smaller, less important aspects we prevent people from getting to heaven to find out the answers.

And here's the main problem;

To a man dying of thirst, water and salt-water both may look the same but only one will save his life.

The gospel is the same simple, pure, clean life saving truth today as it always has been. It's the plain, normal water used to save a man's soul who's dying of thirst.

But sometimes we add so much baggage to that gospel, put so much emphasis on the peripheral things that the plain water gets mixed up. It gets diluted or worse still it loses its ability to be the simple, saving message. It's not always bad things that get added (heck, we're told to be "Salt and light", after all!!) but things get squeezed into the mix that ultimately prevent the life saving water of the gospel from quenching a sinners thirst.

I've seen people put off Christ because they've heard Christians bad-mouthing other churches who do it differently to them. I've seen the church itself made a mockery of in the media because of our divisions. I've seen the simply glass of water, available to save the thirsty mans soul get made undrinkable because of the add-ons we force onto it.

God is big enough for us to worship Him in different methods. We must never forget Jesus' priorities and we must never let the non-essential aspects of the faith cloud out the simple truth of the gospel.

I guarantee that church life would be a lot better if we recognized what the blank spaces meant more and focused our energies and emphasized our priorities just as Jesus did.

Chapter Six
Jesus' Teachings

Well it has been a whirlwind tour! People are being saved left, right and center. Healings, miracles and demon-slaying are becoming the regular routine. The boys and I estimate that there's daily crowds well into their thousands that are now following us around. My sermons have had to constantly shift to suit the differing crowds; some days it's mainly the Pharisees and Sadducees, some days it's 100% sinners. Each get the message but I've had to make sure to change the pitch, the music and the mood-lighting (bonfire-height).

I cannot afford to lose momentum right now and as such Peter's been a great asset by planning out the month in advance. He's booked us into some great venues and has scouted out some cracking support acts to go on before us. He's been amazing on the coal-face too, really good at hyping the crowd up and dealing with trouble-makers.

We've also got ourselves a band! A small group has agreed to go on tour (for a small percent of the daily take) to provide musical entertainment for the crowds and background music while I'm talking. Nothing stirs the soul like a low chord-change to G-minor. Nothing prompts a sinner to salvation like a stirring chorus, repeated twice normally and once a capella.

What I've realized (which I admit I had no idea going into this) is that having a successful mission all boils down to time management. Here's how most of my days break themselves down;

Early Morning:

Wake, eat a hearty breakfast and catch up on the daily Roman gossip (It's important to keep in-touch and relevant so I have a boy who brings me all the latest gossip from Jerusalem). Pray if time allows.

Mid-Morning:

Team meeting. We discuss the previous day and break down the positives and negatives. Regular polls are taken from the crowds regarding their response and constructive criticism. My sermons are subsequently altered according to their results. This has proved invaluable in trimming the fat of my talks and it's this kind of "running ideas up the flag pole and seeing who salutes it" that's really going to take us to the next level when we enter the city next month. Again, pray if time allows.

Lunch:

I tend to get invited out to eat and it's these power-lunches that have helped me seal some amazingly lucrative speaking arrangements for later in the year. Many of the temple officials have laid on lavish banquets for me and the boys (don't worry, we always pack up doggy bags to take back to the crowds!) and it's always useful to be able to reach these guys first because of the immense influence they have.

These guys are the power-brokers. These are the men who have real sway when it comes to spreading the gospel. If we can reach these guys and get them on board, just think how many others will be influenced by their example. If you turn the head the body will follow.

Post-lunch:

This is where things really hot-up. We have another team meeting where we start our "hype" sessions. The boys start encouraging me, telling me stories about what they've seen and how God has moved. We sing together, even dance sometimes. Basically anything that'll get us ready for the big event, whatever gets us "in the moment" and ready for the crowds.

Show-time:

Usually our band goes on first and gets the crowd singing. One of the 3 will then go on to get the crowd warmed up, maybe read a bit of scripture or tell a funny anecdote. Then it's 2 more songs a lighting change, the music lowers and I'm on.

By the time I come to speak the crowds are usually frenzied. They know they're in for a good time and I try not to disappoint.

This is where Johnny B. and I differed. Don't get me wrong, I loved John. But this gospel is one of inclusion not exclusion. Israel has had the tough-father-approach already so now it's time for the gospel of peace. What purpose does it serve to turn crowds away? Why tell them how hard it'll be when that'll only dissuade them. Bums on seats, that's the core focus. Keep 'em coming and eventually they'll come for the right reasons.

With that in mind I make sure to steer the main sermons away from the following areas;

Sin. It's dark, it's boring and it makes people switch off.

Personal issues. I always make sure to keep it generic. I use phrases like "we should really…" and "all of us need to…" rather than focusing on the individual. No one likes being singled out, no one wants to hear from a speaker who makes them uncomfortable.

Judgment. Everyone's got a vague idea about this anyways and it really gives people the willies when I go on about it. I steer clear and talk about "God's love" and the "message of hope" rather than anything dealing with Gods judgment.

Hell. Pretty self-explanatory. I focus on explaining how awesome heaven is going to be instead. No one wants to hear (or could fully appreciate, regardless) how horrendous that place is.

With those exclusions in mind I keep the talk to 20 minutes, max. People have got really low attention spans so I make sure to use lots of props, hand-outs and Scroll-point slides to illustrate my points.

At the end I always make sure to pass around "The List". This is such a vital part of our ministry, I cannot believe other prophets and Rabbis haven't been doing it before. I make the audience sign up and give their addresses so that we can follow them up. If people have been before, they simply tick their names. All Andrew has to do then is look down the list and see whose names haven't been ticked. He then contacts them and asks them why they haven't been back (obviously in a much nicer manner – he's all like, "Hey, we really missed you the other night in Galilee and we were worried that we'd said something that had offended you…". He really does has a gift for this kind of thing).

By using the list, we've decreased our congregational losses by 12% over the past four months and have seen a net increase in visitors inviting their friends by 4%. These figures are far greater than the average Rabbi turnouts and just go to show how much God is doing for us in this ministry.

Post-showtime:

We usually have a quick "hot-debrief" and then a period of wind-down where we just kick back and relax with our rider after the show. There's always a few stragglers and hangers-on but Peter's getting good at spotting them, deflecting them away from me and dealing with their concerns. I've tasked him with running a focus group on whether or not we should set up a dedicated prayer team to take the burden away from him regarding these needy folks and the findings from that group will go into our bi-annual report. This, hopefully, will form part of the discussion at the conference we're planning next year. ("Christ-fest '32" we're planning on calling it).

Late night:

After wind down and after we've grabbed some food and wine it's always nice to mingle with the crowds and get some feedback. Being 100% God I don't need their praise and love them regardless. Being 100% man it's nice to know I'm doing a good job. It's encouraging. I'm about to die for these guys sins so I don't think it's much to ask that I get a "good job, Jesus" or at least a handshake. For this reason I always stand by the door on the way out, so that at least everyone has to give me a handshake.

All of the younger crowd tend to hang out later on and it's so important for me to show my face around their campfires, even if it's just to brush up on the lingo. I may be only 31 but already I feel out of touch with the words these kids are using! If I'm to reach them I have to stay relevant so I tend to relax my tunic, untie my left sandal (it's what they're all doing this season, apparently) and go and chill out with them for a few hours.

After that, it's a bit of journaling (so important to gather ones thoughts) and then straight to bed, ready for another exhausting day tomorrow!!

To be honest, with all that on the schedule, I'm starting to feel like I need to cut back on a few things. I feel like I need to make more "me" time. I haven't spoken to mum in ages or my brothers, and it'd be really refreshing to just go home and see them for a bit. But I know that I'm here to work and that I'm on a tight schedule.

You only have to look at the prophets to see my problem; these guys took years to accomplish what they did. Moses was 40 when he saw the burning bush and he spent another 80 years working for the Lord after that. Isaiah was 30, like me when he started prophesying but the difference is that he carried on like that for 44 years, day-in-day-out after starting his ministry. Jeremiahs prophetic work outlasted 5 different kings! David died relatively young at 70, but he'd been anointed at 25. By my age he was already becoming the greatest king in our history and would carry that on for 40 more years.

These guys were marathon-runners of faith. Their mission lasted their lifetime and those lifetimes were lengthy and full. These guys could afford to take their time, they could write psalms, sing songs and sit back and pray for hours at a time.

I've got 3 years.

3 years to completely change the entire face of human history. 3 years to totally revolutionize everything there is regarding faith, religion and salvation on planet earth. 3 years to cram in words that are going to impact generations, actions which will validate my claims, events that need to take place to solidify my calling and teachings that will form the foundation of the worlds largest church.

1,095 days.

I cannot waste time. I see the people praying in the temple and part of me really does want to be there, wants to have the time to stop and pray. I do miss talking to…myself…but I simply can't waste the time right now. People need saving. The blind need to see. The light needs to shine. I need to keep working.

That's why I've taught the disciples the ultimate "cover-all-bases" prayer. I call it "The Lords Prayer" and you can whistle off that bad-boy in less than a minute if you're really slick. It hits all the major points, goes through all the necessary rigmarole (Adoration – "Hallowed be Thy Name", Confession – "Forgive us our trespasses", Thanksgiving, Supplication etc.etc.) so you know that you're covered for the day.

I've had the boys take a look at it and I'm pretty sure by the end of this current run we'll have skimmed a few lines off and made it even punchier. We're also planning on running up some robes with it stitched on to sell at the larger venues. Merchandise is Johns main focus and he's got some amazing logos already in the works.

And so, with all that said I have to call it a day today. I'm exhausted and we're up early tomorrow to head to Sidon. I need to draft a few sermon changes tonight for the people out there and make a few edits to my speech.

Whoever thought being the son of God would be this tiring!

JR's Response

Well, I don't know about you, but I feel like the Jesus above is some greasy salesman that's doing everything He can to meet His quota by the end of the month. He acts as if there's some sort of incentive program that gives him a bonus with every set of new 100 converts.

And yet the real Jesus couldn't be further from this image.

He didn't do everything in His power to tickle the fancy of the latest crowd to come stumbling up, offering them a good deal in return for their loyalty.

Jesus had a message that He was going to present loud and clear and if you didn't want to get on board or if you didn't understand it (or made no effort to try and understand it) then that was that. Jesus wasn't going to beg and plead with you to follow Him or to buy into what He was saying.

As I've said before, Jesus wanted people who were 100% sold out and committed to Him and the simple Gospel message He spoke about. He didn't want people impressed by fancy buildings, cool light shows, a sweet band, awesome t-shirts or the promise of some incredible giveaways at tomorrow nights show.

And speaking of tomorrow night, that was, as far as I can tell, probably about as far into the future as the disciples had planned out. Probably not even that. I bet if you went and looked at Jesus' diary and His schedule of events in the near future it would probably be fairly empty.

I mean I guess some pages might read "the cross", "the resurrection" and maybe a couple of other big events but other than that it'd be full of blank pages.

Jesus said Himself in the Gospels to not worry about tomorrow for today has enough trouble of its own. He lived by these words, each day to the next.

In James chapter 4 we see a similar idea where James is warning those who plan out where they're going to be tomorrow, next week, next year even. He says "Why, you do not even know what will happen tomorrow." Clearly James had been impressed by Jesus time management skills.

Jesus seemed to be a big fan of taking things one day at a time.

He certainly never really seemed to be in a hurry.

If you really think about that last line for any amount of time at all it should absolutely blow your mind.

He took His time doing things. He started out His ministry by spending 40 days in the desert fasting, praying and preparing Himself for the ministry at hand.

I mean He was pretty tight with God so you think that He could've cranked out His praying and fasting in just a little weekend retreat and then moved on to some other pretty important business to attend to (that whole "saving the world" thing) but He didn't. He took His time.

Jesus the Messiah, who had a limited time to save all of mankind, didn't seem to be in a hurry at all.

I heard a pastor one time put it perfectly. He said, "Jesus the Messiah was the only leader in history to not have a Messiah-complex."

Jesus didn't act like a typical leader. He didn't seem to worry that if He didn't get so much done, every day, in so many places, then everything was going to crumble around down Him.

In fact He seemed to practice just the opposite of this. It is almost as if He didn't want to do everything Himself at all but instead wanted us to be a part of the game plan.

He'd sit down and have dinner with folks, with His boys, with the tax collectors and sinners and would not worry for a second at how long this took.

Let me diverge for a second and deal with that last issue. You may not think that it is that big of a deal that Jesus is recorded as enjoying so many dinners because you're thinking about dinner like we do it; generally at most a 45 minute sprint to the finish so we can hurry and get on with all the other stuff we have going on.

But dinner back then was a journey. It was a time to kick back and relax and enjoy the food and fellowship around you. They literally would recline on pillows, have food and drinks and talk for hours. Dinner was not a sprint for Jesus and his disciples, it was a marathon. It took time out of the day to do. It was a moment of pause, of rest and of enjoyment. And Jesus seemed to relish them.

I compare that mentality to myself and I am quite ashamed. I'll cut dinner short with friends, with family, with my wife or whoever because I have to get back to church and work on my ever-important sermon for the next week.

Jesus never cut dinner short with anyone and He was working on the greatest mission of all-time - salvation for mankind.

Why didn't He work harder?!

Why did Jesus seem to spend a lot of time with unimportant people, doing very "un-mission-orientated" things?!

Wasn't He worried that He wouldn't achieve His goal if He didn't work hard?

Well despite his seeming lack of time management skills He did get stuff done. In fact He achieved more in 3 years than anyone else in history and kick started a complete revolution in belief and attitude in our world. Despite the fact that He acted like a lay about sometimes and didn't seem to seize every opportunity to capture a fleeing soul He ended up saving all of us.

So let's look at the way in which Jesus managed His time. Like I just said, many ministers today (myself included) will cut moments of alone time short. We'll cut time short with family, cut meals short with loved ones, cut conversations short with friends to hurry and get back to "doing ministry", whatever that means to them.

But we're faced with Jesus doing the opposite. He cut time short "doing ministry" to get back to alone time, to time in prayer, to time with His disciples, to time with the lost, and so forth.

I think that Jesus' choice of time management routine can be summed up in 3 headings; Time to rest, Time to pray and Not wasting time.

Firstly then, Jesus loved to rest. Have you ever played the hypothetical game where someone will ask, "if you only had a week to live, what would you do?" Generally there's a fairly generic list you can rattle off, of all the things that you wanted to get done and accomplished.

Now, change that to Jesus' scenario. Imagine it's the last few days of his mission on earth, and He knows He's going to die on a cross that coming weekend. Obviously He doesn't have much time left to spread the Word to everyone and yet what does He do?

He has a final supper with His disciples. He has one of those long meals with His closest friends and fills them in on what is to come.

Despite my generic list, when I really think about it that is how I'd want to go out; one last meal with all my closest friends.

None of this stems from laziness on Jesus' part or on Him ignoring His calling or purpose. Far from it. This was all part of His mission. Jesus was actually more concerned with doing what His Father called Him to do than what His humanity might make Him naturally feel like He should do.

Let me explain;

It's our humanity that tells us to work 90 hours a week if it's for money we don't need.

It's our humanity that has check lists that take priority over people.

It's our humanity that tells us that rest is for the weak and that "real work" is what makes a life worth living.

It's our humanity that wants life to be easier, that "just wants to get stuff done so I can relax" which sometimes, in the process, means we make it a lot harder.

Jesus was 100% human, but He didn't do things like most of humanity

Jesus <u>didn't</u> work 90 hours a week.

Jesus <u>didn't</u> put checklists above people.

Jesus <u>didn't</u> waste effort trying to make life easier because He knew at times that it wouldn't be.

Above all Jesus knew His mission. He knew where He had come from and where He was going. When it came time to speak He spoke with all authority and purpose. When it came time to act He did so with startling love and awesome power. But when it came time to relax He treated that task with just as much due diligence.

The God that rested after 6 days and who forced the Sabbath onto His followers obviously has a penchant and a heart for resting and enjoyment. When the end was near He knew He'd worked as hard as He could and He knew He'd spoken as well as possible. There was nothing left to do but rest.

It's fascinating to see how the human body builds muscle. It's as much performed in the bed as it is in the gym. For all the bicep curls and bench presses we carry out, the real act of building muscle is solidified...in rest. If we don't rest, if we don't let our bodies relax, we burn out. We over train. We get injured.

Jesus put a huge value on rest. As the man, Jesus' body perhaps needed to take a break every now and again but far more so He acted as an example to us, especially in leadership. We cannot always be set on "go". Any bodybuilder will tell you that rest is not wasted time, it's essential.

We need to practice rest – the proper kind of "soul-enriching" rest – as much as we need to practice work. You know that kind of rest I mean, the kind when afterwards you feel refreshed, renewed and reinvigorated. The kind of rest that makes you feel like it's time to start again, pick yourself up, keep going.

Rest is hard, for some. And it's too easy for others! Do not misunderstand me; Jesus wasn't lazy, He wasn't exonerating never working or never getting out there and grafting till it hurts. He was just an advocate of balance, of allowing your batteries to be recharged <u>so that those batteries can be used for something.</u>

As well as this, it shows just how much God enjoys our company. He's a communicative God, a loving God, a companion and someone who can relate to us. He's willing to sit and eat with us, despite His Sovereign status. It's marvelous that Jesus would bother spending so much time just sitting and talking to people. It truly testifies to the character of our God.

As well as rest, Jesus time management encouraged prayer. Now I'll be the first to admit that to me prayer is a weird, awesome, strange, powerful, confusing and incredible thing. The second I try and pin it down, try to figure it out is when it becomes something that drives me nuts.

One thing has become clear in my time in the ministry however; too many of us choose to pray (or choose not to pray) based upon a little scorecard we're keeping in our back pocket. A scorecard of how many times God has actually come through for us from our prayers.

If He has come through for us on repeat occasions and in lots of different circumstances then we'll pray to Him on a regular basis about a lot of different things, ranging from the common, everyday stuff to the big decision, life-changing things.

But if He hasn't come through for us too often then we'll maybe pray at church on Sunday and possibly might say a prayer every now and then as we're dozing off to sleep. Mainly, however, our prayers will be reserved for when we are panicking and we really have nowhere else to turn.

Obviously in reality you have people who fit in all along the spectrum, in and around those two different extremes.

I feel that it is almost like a cause and effect type of thing;

The Cause: God answered my prayer.

The Effect: I will pray more. Not because of God but because <u>I got something</u> out of the deal.

Or;

The Cause: God didn't respond to me and didn't answer my prayer.

The Effect: There isn't a need for me to pray because it <u>just doesn't work</u>.

The problem with all of this is that, basically none of it is Scriptural and none of it is what God had in mind.

Prayer can never be a cause and effect type of thing or something that we do or don't do based upon results. This isn't a credit card rewards program where we pray so many times in a certain period and then God rewards us with a free trip to Paris. This isn't a radio giveaway contest that if we're lucky and we're the 107th caller (or prayer) then we'll win the prize and get our wish.

If you need a blunt reason to pray, it's simple.

Jesus did it.

And you know what? He told us to do it.

Period.

Yep, sometimes things will turn out how we'd hoped they would, and yep, sometimes they won't.

We probably won't ever understand it.

The end.

I did genuinely want to end my contribution right there but I feel like I'd be shortchanging Matt. But what more is there to say?!

I cannot even begin to tell you how many hours of my life I have wasted trying to figure out prayer, trying to dissect it, trying to over-analyze every bit of it, trying to use experience as a guide, trying to rationalize the moving and workings of the Holy Spirit, trying to pin this tragedy on God and His failure to respond to prayers and on and on and on...

But really...Jesus did it. He told me to do it. I had probably just get on and do it.

Jesus experienced the "Yes's" of prayer as well as the "No's". One of those "No's" meant that the cup wasn't taken from Him and that he still had to die. The man knew all about our prayer experiences.

I know that prayer is a powerful, wonderful thing that puts me face-to-face with the creator of the universe, who knows more and sees more than I can ever try and wrap my mind around. Because of that I have to trust that He knows best.

Look at Jesus.

He was the only perfect man to ever live. He was God in the flesh. He saved souls, cast out demons, healed the sick, raised the dead, fed the hungry, gave light to those in darkness, and you know what? He spent a lot of time praying.

Why should I, then, as someone who cant do any of the above, make such a fuss about doing it?!

Was this link to His prayer life mere coincidence?

I think not.

I have no doubt in my mind that one of the main reasons why Jesus was as chilled out about "tomorrow" as we spoke about before and why (despite His maddening urge to stop and eat all the time) He always ended up doing what needed doing was partly down to prayer. I believe it's why He was always somehow led to go where He needed to go, why He was always saying what He needed to say, why He was silent when He needed to be silent and why He went to the cross and died for us all. His life was run with the beating heart of a rich and active prayer life that put Him in conversation with a God who had everything under control.

None of what I'm saying here is about telling you not to work hard. It's about making sure we work hard at the right, fruitful things. One of the most important things to work hard at, is our prayer life.

Jesus knew just how crucial prayer was which is why He gave us a little model to use, with the Lord's Prayer.

And that is just what it is...a model.

On a side note I've always found it interesting that Jesus gave us a model for prayer but not a model for what the church should look like.

Maybe that's because He wanted us, as individuals and as churches to use prayer to help us figure out what our church should look like.

Just a thought...

Anyways, I digress - Christ gave us this prayer to show us what things we need to be praying for and seeking after. It certainly wasn't the only way to pray or the way we had to pray. It was a guide to help us along.

Jesus knows us and knows that without a framework we wouldn't even know where to begin. I mean, think how much we struggle with prayer as it is! Jesus did something incredibly sensible and gave us a black-and-white, a-b-c, 1-2-3 template for prayer. A simple formula for us to use. Imagine how much trouble we'd have if He just told us to pray and then didn't give us any pointers!

We know that it's just a model and a suggestion because Jesus Himself doesn't always do it this way;

In John 17 Jesus spends the whole chapter in prayer. He starts out praying for Himself and then He goes on to pray for His disciples. He then finishes up the chapter praying for future believers.

If the Lord's Prayer was the way to pray then Jesus would have probably thrown it in the mix somewhere in this chapter, but He doesn't. So what is its purpose then?

I am not going to spend a ton of time breaking down the depths of this prayer and all the intricacies of it because there are literally entire books, large volumes that discuss the depths of this and what this prayer means. I am simply going to hit on four big things that I think that this prayer addresses which kind of cover all the bases;

"your kingdom come, your will be done, on earth as it is in heaven"

We are to pray that God's kingdom would come to earth and that His will would be carried out here on this planet, just like it is in Heaven. One could say, in a sense that we are called to strive to bring Heaven to earth by how we live out His will for our lives.

Praying about His will for our lives really taps into a whole realm of things. It has to do with what you do with your day, where you take a job at, where you move your family, what church you go to, where you choose to serve at, what you do with your free time, your struggles with sin and the list goes on.

When we are told to pray "your will be done" then this kind of covers the gamut on how we are to be living our lives, which is why I believe it's so high up in the prayer. It sets the tone for everything else we're going to talk to Him about.

"give us today our daily bread"

This is a simple prayer for provision. It can mean specifically talking about "bread" and our daily food but it is also a lot deeper than that in talking about general provisions for our lives. Everyone, whether poor or wealthy, hungry or well-fed has the question of some types of provision in their world and this calls us to pray to God for these provisions.

It's interesting that Jesus didn't say "give us today a massive bag of cash". It's bread that we ask for. Simplicity. Sufficiency. We ask for what we <u>need.</u> This isn't a Santa list and we're not told to ask for flash cars or new TV's. Jesus could have said anything here but he said "bread".

Now this can cover so many different areas because there are so many different types of provisions out there that people might need, but it's the word "need" that's important.

"forgive us our sin, for we forgive everyone who sins against us"

Forgiveness is something that we all can relate to on many levels.

We've all failed and fallen short and we need forgiveness. We need forgiveness from God and we need forgiveness from those we've hurt in the process. We need to ask forgiveness from family, from friends, from spouses, etc.

We've also been on the other end and had people wrong us. We've had people we love betray us, people we thought were our closest friends turn their back on us, people we confided in tell our secrets to the world and the heartbreaking list can be extensive.

But the deal is that we are called to forgive anything just as Christ forgives us for everything.

This is a simple and challenging call but it one that we all can relate to. It's so interesting that for other people we sometimes want God to be the God of judgment, the God of revenge, the God of "just-desserts" whereas for us we always want the merciful, gracious and forgiving God. We want to receive mercy and forgiveness and yet sometimes find them so hard to give.

"lead us not into temptation"

We need to pray that God would help protect us from those tempting places we tend to put ourselves in. We need His guidance and assistance to help steer us clear of troubled waters where we know we could slip and fall at any given moment.

God, being God, sees and knows more than we ever could. If we're praying for His guidance and help and He sees us strolling down a path that will get us into all sorts of trouble, then He can give us other routes to take.

But when we are not confiding in Him and we are just doing our own thing and living our own life, then before we know it we can be right smack dab in the middle of the lion's den with the devil prowling around looking to devour us.

The reason this is used as a daily prayer is because all of the things listed above are, at the very least, the things we need prayer for on a daily basis;

Daily we need Him to help us be able to live out His will, on earth as it is in Heaven.

Daily we need His provisions to help us get by.

Daily we need His forgiveness and to be willing to do the same for others.

Daily we need Him to guide us and lead us and keep us away from our struggles.

Plain and simple we see from Jesus' example that daily we need to pray.

Lastly, Jesus time management skills emphasized 'not wasting time'.

Jesus did not pussy-foot around. He did not mince His words, or string out vast long prayers like the Pharisees. He was to the point, He was bold, He spoke no-nonsense truths. He didn't waste time trying to sugar-coat things.

This might be one of the areas where we can learn as much as anything.

Some of us need to do a much better job of just being real with people and telling them like it is. We have got to quit being scared that if we are brutally honest with people about the Gospel, about the call of Christ and about what is required of us that they'll turn and walk away. We have to follow the call of being a disciple – that sometimes means we need to be brutally honest about things - and trust that God is bigger than people's fears or worries.

Jesus never chased after numbers. He never watered down His message to make friends or altered His opinions to make things less awkward. Look at the story of the Rich Young Ruler. Look at the story of Mary and Martha. Look at all the other examples when Jesus has to opportunity to paper over an awkward request or to make a lukewarm comment to spare someone's feelings. Does He do it?

Jesus simply told people the truth. He didn't go out of His way to be controversial, wasn't nasty or spiteful and didn't say things just to hurt people but He certainly told people the truth.

How refreshing would it be to know that our ministers and fellow Christians were comfortable enough with losing a few members of the congregation in order to consistently speak the truth? How incredible would it be if we were able to tell people honestly the message of Gods salvation without feeling like we needed to alter it to suit?

Jesus was bold, consistent, honest and upfront. If sin was present, He'd mention it. If people were out of order, He'd address it. If someone asked Him a question, He'd reply, straight up.

Jesus' sense of time management didn't have room for meandering, posturing, waffling or avoiding touching nerves. Yes, He was culturally sensitive and yes He was emotionally savvy when it came to reacting to people but He didn't have time to mess about.

The gospel was told, healings were carried out and then it was back to the local house for a rest!

So, just to recap;

I think Jesus wants us to take our time and enjoy living life with people.

I think He doesn't want us to be in a hurry, thinking its up to us to save the world.

But I also think He doesn't want us to be scared to tell it like it is.

*Most importantly He shows us we should wake up every day and
pray.*

*The more I read about how "if I was Jesus, I would've done it..."
the more I am so thankful that I am called to be like the real Jesus,
not like Matts version. It seems to me that He really knew how to
live life to the full and to get as much out of each day as possible.
That, at the end of the day, is what I want. I think it's what we all
want.*

Chapter Seven
Jesus' Death

The following chapter is taken directly from "MESSIAH-MANIA: The Gospel according to Andrew" released in hardback edition on the day after Jesus' death (to avoid future confusions regarding authenticity)

[12] *And on the first day of unleavened bread, when they killed the Passover lamb his disciples said unto him, "Where wilt thou that we go and prepare that thou mayest eateth of the passover?"*

[13] *And he sendeth forth two of his disciples, and when they hadst returned, saith unto them, "Hast ye found at the very leasteth a Galilee-Holiday Inn, or Jerusalem-Radissons that hast a suitable sized conference room, fine dining and leisure facilities yet at affordable price?"* [14] *And lo there wast much consternation between the 3 until finally Peter spoke up, saying "Nay, I hast initially suggested the Holiday Inn however Andrew wouldst not spendeth the money. He hast instead booked us in at 'The Nags Head' bed andst breakfast".*

[15] *And lo Jesus wept.*

[16] *"Verily this ist to be my final supper with you and yet you could not find us a decent room in a quality establishment? Ist I not the freaking Messiah?! What shouldst we eat for my final meal on earth, cold sausages and egg?! In the 'Nags Head' I imaginst that I have no choice for side dishes and will be forcedeth to have just chips with my main course, ist that correct?" And the three shuffled their feet, diverted their gazes and mumbled "It is as you say."*

"I am saddened." Jesus proclaimed, "I hast deeply desired to spend my last supper in a place that at least had a free salad bar." [17] *And amongst them there was much weeping and gnashing of teeth.*

[18] *And ye, the four of them arrived at the Nags Head and as they sat and did eateth of their cheap steak and soggy chips Jesus saith*

unto them, "Verily I say unto you, I hast bad tidings that I must proclaim to you all."

¹⁹And they began to be sorrowful and to say unto him one by one, "It's the chips, isn't it? And the sub-standard wine. We saideth we were sorry...besides, it was Andrews decision..."

²⁰And he answered and said unto them, "No. I am saddened because of this; the son of man must die, this much is clear to all who understand the scriptures. Therefore must I tell you this; tonight will I perish. After I have put my affairs in order, set out a church-plant vision for the 3 of you, organised your schedules for the upcoming months and arranged my own burial I, the Messiah wilst lie down in our booked room upstairs and wilst haveth a massive, sudden and fatal heart attack.

²¹The Son of man indeed goeth as it is written of him, "And my heart is wounded within me." And yea, though that ist not a direct prophecy...it'll do for this occasion".

²²And then as they did eat, Jesus took Peters hamburger bun, blessed and broke it. Giving it to them he saideth, 'Take, eat: this is my body.'

²³And he tooketh the cup of blackcurrant cordial and when he had given thanks, he gave it to them: and they all drank of it.

²⁴And he said unto them, 'This is my blood of the new testament, which is pumped by my heart. This same heart which is to receive a massive coronary embolism in a few hours time (seest, that actually fitteth in to the prophecy pretty welst, I am most pleased).

²⁵Verily I say unto you, I will drink no more of the fruit of the vine, until that day that I drink it new in the kingdom of God.'

²⁶And when they had sung a hymn, ordered, ate and divided up the cheque along with adequate tip, lo they went out into the mount of Olives.

[27]And Jesus saith unto them, "Take out the slips of parchment I have given you". And verily they all took them out. "Read aloud the words" and verily did they readst them. Jesus continued "Despite the fact that I have told you and even despite the fact that I have written it down for you that I will rise again, ye all shall be tempted to become offended because of me this night. For it is written, 'I will smite the shepherd and the sheep shall be scattered'. I wanted to let you know; if thou moves but a muscle, thou art morons. Don't run away, do as we planned.

[28]Tryeth to remember at leasteth that after that I am risen I will go before you into Galilee. Meeteth me there and bring me a fresh set of clothes and breakfast. I will return"

If you're reading this passage I'm already dead and am writing to you now from beyond the grave. In a few hours' time I'm planning the greatest come-back this world has ever seen but I feel that I owe you an explanation about what just happened.

Let's deal with the elephant in the room first; no, I didn't end up getting crucified.

Hear me out. Let me try and explain. That's not the first time I've had to say both of those things since getting here to heaven, actually.

Look, the important thing is that I did die.

With the 3 around me and with the crowds gathered outside in a silent, candle-lit vigil; with a full belly (even if it was a weak steak) and in a nice bed; with my mum taken care of, my future church securely administrated and with all of my outstanding bills paid I had an enormous myocardial infarction and passed away. End of story. Just as the prophecies (sort of) proclaimed.

"But Jesus you've got to die on a cross…" you'll say. "But Jesus, we Christians have to have the cross as our eternal symbol" you'll yell. Well 'But Jesus' nothing! Do you know how much a crucifixion hurts?! No? Exactly. Well I do, I've seen it happen thousands of times. I'm God, for goodness sakes, why should I have to go through that?!!

You'll probably all have loads of questions and complaints, and so here's my rebuttal to most of them;

1. Scripture says that the son of Man has to <u>die</u>. It doesn't say he has to be <u>executed</u>. Ok, perhaps there's some little prophecy in there somewhere about a tree but all scripture is subjective after all! It can be manipulated! It can be replaced with other verses to suit my eventual end, surely. There are stacks of verses about "broken hearts" and so I'm sure that one of them will fit nicely.

2. Did I take on the worlds sins? Yes. Just before I died I explained to the 3 disciples what was taking place and they relayed the message to the crowds outside. At one point I even sat up and waved to an enormous cheer. Near the end I even faked them out a little just to hear the collective gasp. Anyways, I clearly explained that I was dying for their sins and that I would act as their sacrifice. Then I went ahead and did just that. Dying of a self-induced heart attack is still a sacrifice! It's just not as painful, humiliating and time-consuming as a crucifixion.

3. Why should I have to suffer? The Romans designed crucifixion it's not even a scriptural punishment for sin (not that being stoned would have been much nicer) so why should I have to go along with it? In years to come even the worst offenders and sinners that are dealt with by capital punishment will receive their punishment more swiftly and humanely than being put the cross. Why should the Messiah - the one person in the entire world's history who hasn't offended - be dealt with worse than them?!

4. Let's not forget the fact that I haven't done anything wrong! This is about symbolism not actual judgment, right?! For centuries these people have gotten onboard with the idea about the "scapegoat". Despite the fact that those

goats didn't do anything wrong they symbolically took on peoples sins and received their punishment in their place. I'm just doing the same. Am I dying? Yes. Am I symbolically taking on all of their sins? Yes. So what's the problem?!

5.   More people will believe this way. The whole idea of crowds turning against me while I'm tried as a prisoner is ridiculous – people are going to think that I was a fraud or a failure if I'm suddenly executed. This way I go on my terms and people know exactly what's taking place. No crown of thorns needed, no beatings and no "King of the Jews" sarcasm. I die as the Messiah not as some suspected mad-man. Let's see future generations of atheists try and dispute this one!

6.   My disciples and my parents and family don't have to experience the humiliation and trauma this way. I've explained it all to them. I'll always be remembered as a hero (saving my mum the social stigmatism of having a son executed) and the disciples are now well prepared for a future as apostles. None of this "Forgive them Father, for they don't know what they're doing" rubbish. They now know exactly what I just did for them and they know exactly what to do now.

7.   Ok, ok, so I know that we've now lost the image of the cross. What will people wear around their necks and have as nasty-looking tattoos now? I'll tell you what - I commissioned an artist to portray me in my last moments as I'd like to be remembered. Not the weak, frail, beaten man on the cross but as the powerful son of God bravely accepting humanities sins on his shoulders and stoically laying down on his hotel bed to endure 30 seconds of pain for each and every one of them.

Basically it looks like me smiling and flexing both biceps together. It's still kind-of in the shape of a cross so it'll still work as a piece of jewelry for teenagers and rock-stars only this time it'll have a much nicer appeal than the cross. Who wants to wear a symbol of capital punishment anyways?!

8.   Dying this way also prepares the way for a much more verifiable resurrection. Having invested some of the money that we'd made on tour I've purchased a grade-A tomb and have distributed flyers in each show highlighting its location and opening times etc. The disciples have been briefed about the next stage and they should already be setting up the banners around the tomb for my return.

I know it may seem like I copped out but I'm being honest here - through all of this one thing has been recurrently going around in my head; why should I make it difficult for people to believe?

That's the root of all of my issues with the "old way" that was planned out for me. Why make it hard?

- Why make it seem like my mission had failed by turning crowds away with tough teaching?
- Why annoy the Pharisees when by getting them on side I could reach more of their congregations?
- Why frustrate the Romans by having a parade into Jerusalem?
- Why make it hard for future believers by having me executed like a common criminal?
- Why make it tough for my disciples by having them put under pressure themselves when they start setting up my church?
- Why ruin all this good publicity that I've had so far by making the resurrection so low-key.

Let's not forget that I am God, after all! I've never really had a problem with self-promotion before. I sent floods, pillars of fire, burning bushes, plagues, devastation, manna, crumbled city walls, gave men super strength, wrote on walls, saved people from lions; why should I suddenly be so coy, especially as this is my big moment!!!

It's all about people believing that I just died in their place. Why shouldn't I make it easy for them? Would you really rather believe in someone who said they were the son of God and who was then brought in for questioning by your authorities and subsequently executed by them, obviously highlighting their guilt? Is that someone you'd really want to follow? Surely it just leaves too many questions unanswered that way. This way it's cut-and-dry.

I died as the Messiah. I've died at the top of my game; people know the reasons why and are at fever-pitch expecting my return. It's the best way for all. Mission Complete.

JR's Response

Ok, I guess this is the point in this book where things get real. No preamble, no messing around, here's why Jesus did it His way;

Jesus' death is the pinnacle of His ministry and the whole reason why God became man. Everything He did led up to it and I believe it had to go down the way it did. Specifically, the cross. The reasoning behind it breaks down into three different categories;

Scriptural.

Cultural.

Theological.

Let's start by looking at the scriptural reasoning. To be honest, this is kind of the easiest and most obvious one to explain because all I need do is reference the Old Testament.

Jesus' life was not a random chain of events. He was not just some guy who happened to live in a random country and who was born in a random town at a random time in human history. His life, in some aspects, was predictable.

Most of His life was fulfillment of prophecies that had been written centuries before. Prophecies regarding His coming riddle the Old

Testament. Huge events such as His birth and being born of a virgin in Bethlehem, right down to small, seemingly trivial things like riding into town on a donkey were all predicted in prophecies.

This implies that there were reasons why He was born how and where He was, why He came from the line of people He came from, why He did the miracles He did etc. His life ticked off the prophecies, even the ones He had no control over. His life was a steady completion of what the Old Testament had been forecasting for hundreds of years.

Scholars will say that there are over one hundred predictions and prophecies of the Messiah's coming and that Jesus fulfilled every single one of them. In fact the odds of a random guy fulfilling just a handful of these predictions would be something like 1 in 100, billion, billion, billion.

Therefore if His life was fulfilling predictions – what about His death?

Well it too was no random event, happening at some random time of the year in front of a random bunch of folks who had just happened to get caught up in the random moment and had joined in with the whole "crucify him, crucify him" thing.

All of the Old Testament, all of human history in fact had led up to this moment, and the prophecies were fairly clear on how it had to happen.

Everything about the crucifixion, from somewhat vague things like being rejected by the Jews (Psalm 118:22) and dying a humiliating death (Isaiah 53) to highly detailed specifics like being spit on (Isaiah 50:6), piercing His hands and feet (Psalm 22:16) and dying with no broken bones (Psalm 34:20) were predicted beforehand.

As a side note, what is pretty unique about the "no broken bones" thing is that this would have been a fairly difficult one to fulfill because it was a common practice to break the legs of those being crucified to speed up their death. Jesus, however, was already dead when the soldiers came around to check on them and so there was no need (John 19:32-33).

Here are some more prophecies that were fulfilled...

- Jesus would be betrayed for 30 pieces of silver (Zechariah 11:12-13)
- Jesus would be silent before accusers (Isaiah 53:7)
- He would be killed with other criminals (Isaiah 53:12)
- The gruesome crucifixion foretold (Psalm 22)
- casting lots for His clothes (Psalm 22:18)

My point is then firstly, without even looking into anything deeper than simple Scripture, it's clear that Jesus dying on the cross was the final part of all the things that had to happen to Him in order to fulfill what was prophesied in the Old Testament.

There is no way that the Messiah, Jesus Christ, could have died from a heart attack or by getting hit by an out of control chariot or falling into a well or by contracting leprosy or any other means of death. It had to be the cross; the Old Testament was pretty clear about it.

But even this, even the reason of "fulfilling the final prophecy" doesn't settle the reason <u>why</u>. Why couldn't they have prophesied something easier for Him? Why did it have to be crucifixion?

Let's look at the next reason why it had to happen this way. There was also a cultural implication behind it happening the way it did.

The Jewish leaders wanted Jesus dead, period. If you read the gospels it's clear that behind all their questioning, all their charades and pretense they wanted this upstart killed. They desperately wanted to find a way to trip Him up, have Him break a law or do something against the Romans and then kill Him for it. And Gods law was their excuse.

The problem was though that even if they could get someone to betray Him and get their crew behind it all it still was not entirely up to them. Even as a law-breaker Jesus wasn't in their hands to punish.

At the particular time in history when Jesus was going to be put on trial for all his "crimes" Palestine was being ruled and run by the Romans. Now in many ways the Romans let the local folks handle their business the way they were used to handling it but they would not allow the local rulers to dish out the death penalty. Therefore even when the Jews got all their cards in play they were not allowed to be the ones to put Jesus to death.

All they could do was take Jesus to the Roman governor at the time, Pontius Pilate, and then do their best to persuade him to give the go-ahead for Jesus' death. And they certainly tried (and succeeded) with Pilate finally bowing to public pressure.

What's amazing is that it's in this little side-stepping that the Jews had to do which led to another prophetic fulfillment.

If the Jews had been able to impose the death penalty on their own then they would have gone ahead and looked back at their guidelines, given by God in the Old Testament. What they would have found written, and then subsequently carried out was Jesus being stoned to death.

Had this happened, then all the prophecies about Jesus hanging on a tree, having His hands and feet pierced, having His side pierced, being offered vinegar and gall to drink, not having any broken bones, being executed with other transgressors, etc., would not have been fulfilled.

Only because the final verdict was in the hands of the Romans and only because crucifixion was happened to be their way of execution, were the prophecies ultimately fulfilled.

Crazy, huh?! The Old Testament, thousands of years earlier prophesied that one day the Jews would be an occupied people!

And yet still even this cultural understanding of the root cause of Jesus' death being a Roman crucifixion and not a Jewish stoning doesn't explain <u>why</u>. We still aren't any closer to understanding ultimately why Jesus had to be <u>killed</u> and not just <u>die.</u>

Actually the question of why Jesus had to die this way, why He had to be executed has a very deep and hard to take-in theological reason.

Simply put, humanity is a sinful bunch. The bible is as clear about this as it is about anything. Right from the early days in the Old Testament God sets out the law. Why? To show us just how sinful we are. If this fact hasn't quite sunk in for you, let me spell it out clearly (bearing in mind that this might get a bit rough);

I have on many occasions had people come up and say to me "I'm not that bad a person". "I haven't killed anyone" or "I haven't committed adultery", "I mean, I'm not <u>that bad.</u>"

And that's fantastic. I'm glad there aren't more murderers out there. Chances are that you too reading this are probably not a killer or an adulterer. But the fact is that if you're basing your idea of being "good" on a scale with events like murder or adultery, then you're using the 10 commandments as your benchmark. And therein lies the problem. Those sins are only at positions 6 and 7 on the list...and so what about the rest?

If you're going to use Gods law to decide if you're a good person or not, what about law number 1? What about the commandment "I am your God, worship no one but me". Have you broken that one?

Or what about number 4? Sure, you've not killed anyone but have you always kept the Sabbath sacred? Or number 5? Sure you've stayed faithful to your wife or husband but have you <u>always</u> honored your mother and father?

The problem with saying "I'm not that bad" or "I'm not a sinner" is that you are tripped up by the very thing that you're using to define your own goodness – Gods law. It's not enough to keep some of it to call yourselves "good"; only someone who can keep all of it is that.

If we really want to hammer the point home, take Jesus' own example. What does He say is the most important commandment?

"Love the Lord your God, with all your heart, soul, mind and strength."

Have you kept that?

Me neither. And so I'm a sinner. I'm a law breaker. Heck, I cant even keep the most important commandment let alone the smaller ones. I've broken Gods law and I'm not alone, far from it.

The bible clearly states that;

"We all have sinned and have fallen short of the glory of God"
(Romans 3:23)

And so here is the issue. We are suddenly faced with a rather large elephant in the room; our sin.

God made a covenant with His people and within this covenant there were rules and requirements; a whole bunch of do's and don'ts that He required His people to obey.

Back when these rules were given God was very clear about the consequences or our actions. If you did what was asked of you then you were blessed. If you disobeyed and went about your own way then you were cursed.

Tying these two parts of the bible together it becomes clear that if "we all are sinners" and if anyone who sinned was cursed, then according to the covenant <u>we are all cursed</u>. It states this in Deuteronomy 27:26 and reiterated in Galatians 3:10.

Us being cursed creates a pretty sizeable problem.

The deal is that God hasn't changed in His reaction to, or opinion of our sin. As a perfect God and as a perfectly just God, sin still has to be punished. Just as it was in the Old Testament a price has to be paid, a penalty meted out for our sin and a curse still has to be given.

Without this there is no way that we, as imperfect, sinful beings could ever enter the presence of God or be in good standing with Him. Somehow right from the start of our relationship with God, there has always had to be some way for the penalty of our sin to be paid.

There are many ways to look at our sin and many different phrasings that are used to describe humanity's sin in relation to Jesus and to God.

Sometimes our sin is referred to as a debt that has to be paid. Obviously this raises an instant problem, however. How do I pay? What do I have to pay with? How can I get out this debt?

Sometimes our sin is seen as a demonstration of enmity between God and us. We have sullied the relationship by living life how we desire as opposed to what He desires for us. Again this poses a huge problem; as an enemy of God we are not in good standing with Him and therefore how can we fix the relationship with Him?

A last way that sin is sometimes viewed is that it is a crime against God. There had been an established and expected way that we were supposed to live, filled with commands and laws and we have broken them. As lawbreakers however, how do we atone for our crimes? How can we take back what has already been done?

When we look at any one of these, or at all of these combined we see immediately how hopeless the scenario might appear for all of us.

How can we get out of the red, with insurmountable debt?

How can we get in good standing with God when we regularly do things that keep us in bad standing?

How can we escape punishment for crimes that we keep on committing?

How can we fix this?

The only answer is...that we cant. There's no way out of this, there's no way for us to sort this situation out. We deserve punishment. In fact as breakers of Gods law we deserve Gods laws punishment: death.

But (and that's probably the most important 3 letters in the entire history of the world, right there!) as you might have guessed this is where Jesus on the cross comes in to play.

In order for humanity to even have a shot at surviving, let alone have a chance at a relationship with God, death has to happen. A punishment fitting the crime. An act of legal justice, of ultimate execution and of final payment for the sins of the sinner.

What it ultimately boils down to is that either I have to be killed for my sins or else Jesus did.

Jesus could, and probably would have chosen the heart attack. It's because of my sins that He was given the cross.

It's not that Jesus needed to be executed; it's that I needed to be.

As a lawbreaker my sins needed to be killed, not just to die. We cannot overlook this fact. What we do, what I do on a daily basis as sins in the eyes of God are what nailed Jesus to the cross. My sin is despicable to God and it is a costlier price to pay than just a heart attack. My sin is a crime whose only punishment is execution.

And that's only my sin! Jesus died for all of our sins! The only price that could be paid for all of that sin was the only son of God.

Someone who stood in the middle between God and humanity had to take the punishment that we all deserved.

Fortunately for mankind, this is exactly what Jesus did.

He was God in human form who lived life 100% as a man but He did so in an absolutely perfect way, without any sin.

Only because of this could Jesus be a sacrifice costly enough to pay off all of our debt.

He could be the mediator that fixes the relationship between us and God.

He could be the one who is punished for our crimes.

He could be the ransom that was paid for our transgressions.

And so this is exactly what happened, Jesus became the substitute for us. He became the one to take away the sins of the world (John 1:29).

Only on the cross could all the sin of the world, all the mistakes of humanity and all the blemishes of mankind be transferred to Jesus and summarily executed. Only on the cross could the wrath of God be poured out for the horrendous multitude of sins we commit. Only on the cross could the curse of humanity fall upon Jesus and be nailed put.

Galatians 3:13 says that, "Christ redeemed us from the curse of the law by becoming a curse for us, for it is written: "Cursed is everyone who is hung on a tree.""

It is for these reasons why we see Jesus ask the tragic question, "My God, my God, why have you forsaken me?"

Only on the cross could Jesus become like man, "cursed on a tree" in a separated standing with God and held up as an enemy. For the first and only time in His life Jesus was truly alone at this point.

God had to look the other way because our sins were on His shoulders.

The cross was <u>absolutely</u> imperative for mankind. It was the only way for our sin to be rightly punished and for us to find favor with God, to be able to stand in His presence some day.

Scripturally we see that it had always been foretold as crucifixion. Culturally we can see the reasons why it had to be particularly that method. But only theologically do we really understand the reason <u>why</u>. Crucifixion was the only way for us to have a shot in hell...actually, the only way for us to have a shot out of hell...to be saved. Jesus didn't need to be killed, <u>our sin did</u>

Chapter Eight
Jesus' Resurrection

It's amazing that sometimes, despite all the best intentions and motives, things just don't seem to work out the way you planned them. Going into this I had this whole resurrection thing scripted to the nth degree. I knew all the ins and outs, the pitfalls and traps. I'd planned for every eventuality and prepared my staff and myself for my incredible first-coming. And yet it turned out so vastly different from my intentions that I...well I'm confused.

Rule #1 of my mission was simple; people need spectacle. That's obvious to anyone who has spent any time in the entertainment industry. People want a bit of intrigue, a bit of suspense, a bit of mystery, yes. Definitely. But at the end of all of that they have to get some bang for their buck. They need a payoff and that's what we gave them.

Let me explain;

I gave it a week, being dead. It took that long to whip up interest in some of the outlying areas, to build the stage area, to arrange transportation for the crowds and to distribute our literature explaining what was happening. We also had to wait for our permit applications to run past Pilate and to pay off the Roman guards to allow this all to take place.

Once we were ready, however it all went smoothly. The tomb was laid out as directed, the stage was set and the tiered seating arranged tightly around it. At the designated time, once night had fallen a single candlelight was shone onto the stage and the audience hushed. Stepping out slowly Peter made his way into the light and began to pray, his voice echoing through the quiet crowd. Steadily he recited the prayer we'd written together;

Almighty Father God above,
Looking down from up on-high,
Please send your Spirit like a dove,
And raise the son you sent to die.

Slowly, behind him the band began to play. Their harmonizing voices providing a steadily rising crescendo behind Peters words;

Don't leave us hanging out to dry,
Don't make us all look fools,
Prove that Jesus was your guy,
And that His Kingdom rules.

Give us a miracle; pop our eyes from our sockets,
Pour out love to conquer hate,
Let these people dig into their pockets,
To fill our collection plates.

With that the volunteers appeared, jingling the wooden bowls. The candles that were given out to the crowds were lit and people started waving them above their heads as the music rose louder;

You gave Him strength, filled up His cup,
Stirred Him when He felt low,
So come on now and raise Him up,
These people came to see a show.

The local children we'd hired started miming out their interpretations of my miracles around the stage, the best child-actor we'd found sitting in a make-shift bed in the center, mimicking my death. Peter stepped to the edge of the stage, his voice now booming above the thundering music;

Don't let us down; don't let this be over,
Don't make me sound a liar,
Come on now you big Jehovah,
And prove you're God with FIRE...

At that point the real stage-show began. The trails of oil that the stage hands had poured out were lit from backstage, burning up in an arc towards the candle-lit tomb. Even from inside I could hear the crowds "oohs" and "aahs" at the display and waited to hear Andrews knock, signaling it was time to make my entrance.

The children cleared the stage, the flames now flickering over Peter's face, the entire crowd transfixed by this vast spectacle. All other candles were blown out, the only light coming from the glowing arc of fire. In hushed tones my top disciple finished his prayer, closing his eyes for effect and dropping to his knees;

He came for me and he came for you,
Came to heal and save,
But now its time, so if you need the loo,
Please hold it, just be brave.

Cos now it's time, now we receive,
Your son, into light from black.
We surely all must now believe,
And so it's Jesus-time…Welcome back!

I heard the second set of knocking on the tomb wall and knew it was time. Heaving, splitting the heavy rock into pieces, I stepped from its ashes into the spotlight and performed my signature bicep-flex. The fires light cast a vast silhouette of my shape onto the sheet we'd strung up behind me (handily it also fell on the emblem of our tunics that were for sale at the back) and for a split second there was silence.

Then the crowd went wild. I have never heard a noise like that, outside of heaven. Only the Roman guards we'd paid kept them from rushing forwards to me and a few squabbles and fights broke out initially. Walking from left to right I milked the applause for all it was worth before eventually managing to calm them down, hushing them into silence before speaking;

"Ha ha ha…well then…it sure is good to be back."

A roar of approval went up and I took my second bow. Some people threw flowers, others rushed forwards again, the burly guards barely able to push them back from the stage.

"People, people this is just the beginning. Sin is dead."

Another roar, or at least more spill-over from the first round of applause. I did start to wonder at this point if they were actually listening but I could see their faces. Squirming, thrashing, the elation was obvious.

"The old way has gone, the new has arrived. It's time for you all…to believe"

At that cue John unlocked the cage and released the doves which fluttered upwards, past my outstretched arms and into the sky to further rapturous applause. Which went on. And on. And on and on. As the night wore on it became the spectacle that the moment deserved. The son of man had returned. This was earth's turning point. The band played, people sang, voices and choruses lifted up towards the sky for nearly an hour. The crowd joined in and then the children returned and acted out some skits that they'd rehearsed. For hours we partied like there was no tomorrow. There had never been a night like it in living memory, no returning army or conquering king was ever welcomed back so well. All in all it was an occasion fit for the Lord.

Eventually though, when the pandemonium had calmed down I finished off the teaching I'd been trying to slot in around all the hype;

"So remember friends, this is only the beginning. I will be appearing throughout the next month at the locations listed on your hand-outs and I want to see all of you there. Bring your friends, bring your families and bring your neighbors. All are welcome. Ladies and gentlemen, the King…is back"

The rest of that day became a blur of interviews, public appearances, clamoring crowds, rushed handshakes and autographs. I managed to do a few more healings but, to be honest it was a whistle-stop trip straight up through the city to Pilate.

This was the man that I needed to see if I was really going to break through to the lost. This guy held the keys to the city and I knew that if I could make him into a believer, my way into Jerusalem, Rome even, would be secure.

I ended up meeting with him and his wife, eating with them and regaling them with stories about my appearances, my miracles and my death. From the massive high that was the resurrection moment I have to admit that this meal was quite a crashing come-down.

Initially he seemed skeptical especially regarding the heart attack, and I realized quickly that I should have picked a more visible method of death. At least with crucifixion I could have shown him the scars or displayed the wounds. I realized a heart attack was relatively easy to fake. Eventually I was forced to call in a few witnesses to give their testimonies before he reluctantly agreed to think about what I had said.

That was a shock. I couldn't believe it. I should have given him some VIP tickets to the resurrection itself; it was a glaring administration error for which I berated Peter afterwards. If only he'd have been at the gig I'm sure he'd have believed. Perhaps we should have made more seating available or perhaps we should have arranged a resurrection tour. I just naturally assumed that everyone who'd been at the resurrection would go home and spread the news, tell others about how amazing it had been and convince them to believe.

And so I have to admit, I was a bit disappointed with Pilate. I really thought he'd have been swayed by the public response. The crowds were beating outside his door, his own personal guards having to wrestle with a few desperate souls who just wanted to catch a glimpse of me and yet he seemed to view me with nothing more than suspicion. Perhaps he felt threatened. Perhaps it was jealousy, I don't know.

Leaving him and his wife a little dejected I headed back to the stage area to find more of the crowds still milling around. Getting back on stage I tried to talk to them more about Gods Kingdom, to explain the truth about why I had risen. By that point however it proved frustratingly stunted. People didn't seem to want to listen they were just screaming and yelling, some fainting or ranting wildly at me. They kept yelling at me to perform, to heal, to do something flashy. When I started trying to talk to them about becoming fishers of men I even heard some people booing, jostling forwards and getting nasty.

In a moment things changed. Punches were thrown and Andrew was crushed by some of the crowd, his cries quickly drowned out amongst the throngs of people all screaming at me. In the end I had to quickly pray for a thunderstorm, the beating rain driving them back and dampening their rage.

I ducked out around a few back streets and the disciples and I took refuge in Peter's mother's house. All four of us sat in damp silence, looking out at the rain hammering down on the remnants of the stage in the distance, washing the stage props into the broken and empty tomb. All in all it wasn't exactly the response that I had expected.

What had we done wrong? I thought people said that they'd believe me if they saw it with their own eyes. People had always moaned at my Father that He'd been too quiet, that if only He'd appeared more or put on more of a show they'd be able to believe.

I thought people would be more inclined to listen, more attuned to hearing about Gods plan for them when I spoke if I'd given them what they wanted. I thought, above all else that by giving them the spectacle of resurrection everything that I'd spoken to them over the past 3 years would suddenly be solidified in their hearts.

This was supposed to be the final miracle, the icing on the cake, the seal on the envelope. My return was supposed to be the crescendo, the point at which people truly believed. But as it turned out over the next few week's things went from bad to worse. Getting over the initial disastrous setback I genuinely figured that the following shows would still be packed. The numbers that turned up at my shows did start strong but as I started focusing on sermons more than healings the numbers dwindled and eventually dropped off drastically.

Eventually I realized why. I had heard the stories about someone else in Corinth who was also proclaiming to be the Messiah and now, evidently he was also saying that he'd been brought back from the dead. He had a few party tricks - a neat little gimmick with some wires even had me fooled for a moment - and most importantly he kept up the "magic show" night after night. This guy ended up stealing at least half of my crowd who all flocked to watch him. He even offered them little vials of water which he said "held his heavenly tears" and which would "heal all sicknesses of those who drank it". Man I wish I'd thought of that. Maybe that's what I was missing, better merchandise.

He also made a fortune from these - they cost nearly a denarii each – and people were buying them like crazy, hanging them round their necks and pouring them into their wines at mealtimes. People soon moved on from him too though. First to another "miracle worker" in Philippi who had a pet monkey with him (that was supposed to be able to cure dropsy by dancing) and then over to a new guy in Galatia who claimed he could fly.

I realized that the old "bread and wine" I'd talked about at the last supper just weren't catchy enough and so, I'm ashamed to admit for a short while I attempted to win some of the crowds back by offering small blocks of wood – parts of the bed I'd died in – as holy relics for their houses. It didn't work. Evidently, these other "Messiahs" must have had better PR agents than me.

And so here I am, nearly a year after R-day and we've just reached another new low. Andrew's just given me his resignation notice. Andrew! One of my closest and dearest employees has told me he's been given a better offer by one of the other guys and is moving over in four days to head-up their Ephesus division. I'm stunned. I'm the real Messiah! He knows that, he's seen everything I've done and been with me all along. Why won't people believe? Maybe we need to send another flood.

I really thought that this was my big moment. I really thought this was going to be it, my Fathers Kingdom on earth, my mission complete, sinners saved and souls scavenged.

163

My resurrection was to be a savior's homecoming. A Messiahs return and a moment of such overwhelming emotional response that whole nations were to be converted. Kings would believe and line up with paupers. Emperors saved hand-in-hand with the homeless and the spotless sitting with sinners.

Perhaps people thought it was a trick. Perhaps people just got bored with me. For whatever reason this just hasn't worked out the way I expected it to. Which is why I'm back here where I began, carving a table for Cyrus for some money and living back with mum. I still get the royalties from the gospels every now and again but I'm pretty sure this wasn't the way it was meant to be.

But I haven't given up. I'm the Messiah. I died for people's sins; I'm not planning on fading away. Which is really why I've written all of this down. You see I'm planning something else. Something bigger. Something that's going to blow the roof off and bring everyone I've lost back.

It's going to be huge, a "Messiah 2.0" so to speak. More spectacle, more oomph, more glitz, glamour and glory. All I need is your support. And so if you're interested please contact me. All you need to do is send 4 denarii for an administration fee and you can join my rapidly growing team of volunteers. Why not become my disciple and let's try this again. Let's really focus on spreading the good news of my death and resurrection amongst the lost. This time around we'll be cooler. We'll be slicker. We'll call ourselves something catchy that the 20-somethings will be into. This time we'll make people listen, this time it has to work.

You haven't heard the last of Jesus Christ. I'll be back. Again.

JR's Response

Simple truth; if Matt was Jesus...heck if I was Jesus...the world would not have been saved.

That's the conclusion of this book, right there.

If I was Jesus mankind would not have had the chance to change and life as we know it would not be, well, life as we now know it.

What we see in this chapter is a final, clear and perfect example of how different the real life, death and resurrection of Jesus was from everything that "God's people" had experienced in the past.

Throughout this book we have seen this straightforward picture of a Savior and of a God who did not do things at all like we would today and this is especially true when it came to His resurrection.

When I say this I am not just talking about how we as regular, mortal, sinful humans would do things; I am talking about how we as the universal Christian church would do things. Even us godly folks would screw this part up, especially.

As ever, Christ did it differently.

In the real resurrection, the way it truly went down we see a little bit of just about everything we have talked about so far;

In His baptism we saw how Jesus was not about being seen as a 'big show' or about being in the spotlight, and now we see the resurrection as this quiet, reserved event, seen by only a few.

In His temptation we saw that Jesus had the chance to do things differently; to choose an easier path of recognition, fame and power, and yet chose the higher call. In the resurrection, the final chance for Him to reveal His awesome power and might we see a very upside-down response instead. One of quietness and secrecy.

In the choosing of the disciples we saw how the Messiah and hope for mankind chose folks who the religious world would never have considered, and in the resurrection we see the Messiah appear to the same kind of folks first.

In the prodigal son story we see a Father who loves unconditionally. Even though His son had run off and turned his back on him he welcomed him home with open arms. In the resurrection we see the unconditionally loving Jesus welcome back with open arms the folks who had turned their backs on Him, who'd run off and abandoned Him.

We've seen how Jesus did not tell us how to run church, how to schedule our day and how life should play out exactly, and after the resurrection we see Jesus leave an expectant mankind still without all the answers.

We've seen how Jesus gave us the basics for prayer and what we should be concerned with but not a black-and-white how-to list, and in the resurrection we see how Jesus left them only with the basics, still leaving a huge amount of things up in the air.

And finally on the cross we saw a very vulnerable Jesus challenging everything that His people had ever been told to believe about the Messiah's coming. We saw a savior sacrificed, a God nailed to the cross and then in the resurrection, once again we see the same humbleness, the same challenge for believers, the same emphasis on faith.

The deal is that even as it happened, the resurrection cannot be made more monumental. It is the most essential act of all of our lives.

The bible is split down the middle; the Old and New Testaments each taking a side. One group of books and letters followed by another group of books and letters. The book itself is clearly marked as changing from one to the other at the end of Malachi and the start of Matthew.

But perhaps the real divide was at the resurrection. Perhaps at the end of Matthew 27 a nearly blank page needs inserting, just simply reading "ACT 2".

Although they are called the "old and new testaments" I feel as if they could almost be renamed as the "old way of doing things" and "the new way of doing things". The resurrection is the start of the new things. In fact the resurrection itself is one giant picture of these new way of doing things.

Through much of the Old Testament God was all about spectacle. It sounds like a something a preschooler would write but in the Old Testament He was a very big God. We read constantly about how He was very present in our world and was a very active and visible God.

Just look at so many of the very big things that He did;

- blowing up entire cities with burning sulfur (Genesis 19)
- bringing crazy plagues on the land (Exodus 8-12)
- leading His people with a pillar of cloud and fire (Exodus 13)
- parting the Red Sea (Exodus 14-15)
- raining down manna and quail from Heaven (Exodus 16)
- sending a bunch of snakes to punish the Israelites (Numbers 21)
- talking out of a donkey (Numbers 22)
- making the sun stand still in the sky (Joshua 10)
- using Sampson to kill a thousand men with the jawbone of a donkey (Judges 15)
- using a little shepherd and a slingshot to slay a giant warrior (1 Samuel 17)
- bringing down fire from Heaven and destroying false prophets (1 Kings 18)
- letting Jonah live inside a whale for three days (Jonah)
- rescuing three guys from a fiery furnace (Daniel 3)
- stopping a hungry den of lions from touching Daniel (Daniel 6)
- appearing regularly to folks in dreams, visions or by sending angels.

The list goes on and on.
In the "old way of doing things" we see a God who is very visible, who is tangible, who is spectacular and who was doing everything in His power to show everyone that He was the all-powerful, all-mighty, God of the universe.

And you know what? It didn't seem to really work that well at changing people's hearts.

167

Look at the Old Testament. Look at the Israelites; God repeatedly showed Himself to His people in more miraculous ways than have ever been done since and, although for a little while the people were on board, as soon as God stepped back and turned off the lights the people just went about their business as normal.

I apologize for another list but anyone who has read the Old Testament knows the trend;

1. God shows Himself to His people
2. The smoke and lights catch people's attention
3. They like the cool show so they jump on board
4. God slows down the circus and leaves them on their own
5. Things don't go well for a moment
6. The people start to whine, lose interest and end up falling away, building a golden cow or turning their back on God
7. God gets upset with them
8. He does something huge and monumental that shocks them
9. Rinse and repeat

What I'm about to say is not theological or biblical, but here is what would have gone through my mind as the God of the Old Testament;

"Are you guys kidding me? I've done everything for you. I give and I give and I give and not only are you always ungrateful, but the second I turn my back you go off and do your own thing! I've tried everything, what more do you want?!

I gave you a perfect garden to live in; it wasn't enough. I saved you from slavery; not enough. I rained down food on you from heaven; you whine. I repeatedly save you from enemy forces; you chase after their gods. I've altered astrological events for you, I've given you every kind of leader you've wanted (judges, priests, kings), I've conquered nations with you, given you the law, prophets, miraculous proof of my existence and love for you and yet nothing is enough! This cannot go on!"

Fortunately I doubt God was thinking that. Except for the last sentence. Because the truth of the matter is that it didn't go on. It was never intended to go on. He was always going to send Jesus and then one day, He did.

Jesus came to do things differently, as we have seen throughout this book, and the reason He did was because God wanted our response to Him to be based upon something different than the old ways.

The Israelites were, perhaps, guilty of following God because of His actions. Notice the plural. He was a God that showed up and did incredible things for them. Truly amazing things. But perhaps they treated Him like the genie He definitely wasn't. They were there with Him during the show-times and perhaps they wanted to put Him back in the bottle afterwards.

But really God has never wanted us to follow Him just because we like the show. As such the resurrection wasn't just 'one more performance' that He used to try and sway His wayward followers, it was the final act. Jesus himself was proof that God no longer wanted us to follow Him just because of His actions. He wants us to follow Him because of His one, final action; Jesus resurrection. He is it. His death is it. His resurrection is it. The truth is that if God no longer does anything else in my life then I still owe Him everything because of that one action. Nothing more needs doing.

God no longer wants us to follow Him because He has provided us manna, He doesn't want us to follow Him because He appears in a cloud of smoke and solves all our problems, He doesn't want us to follow Him because of what He can do for us and He doesn't want us to follow Him because we're supposed to because of our lineage or cultural heritage.

It's all about an action; the resurrection. None of the power of the cross itself would be possible without the resurrection.

169

In the resurrection we see God finally (in some respect) making it easy for people. Let's be honest; He could have left it with Jesus hanging there, nailed to the cross and it'd still be a life changing story. He could have left it with Jesus in the tomb and it'd still have convinced some people. He could have asked us to believe in just that part of it but the amazing thing is that He didn't.

Buddha didn't rise from the dead. Mohammed didn't either. Jesus did. It's the show-stopper. The cross isn't the punch-line, the resurrection is. It's the best news for mankind and it's what changes Jesus' life from a myth that has some decent moral code behind it into something that genuinely can save your soul for eternity.

In the amazing film "The Prestige" Michael Caine describes 3 parts to a magic trick (and stick with me here, I'm not in anyway saying that the resurrection was magic!) that people need to happen to be truly amazed; the setup, the performance and finally the prestige, or effect.

His character says that people can be impressed if you leave it just at the performance point (in his example, making a bird disappear) but in order to truly amaze them, "you have to bring it back". There has to be a final effect. A woman, sawn in two and then brought back together. A vanished man reappeared. A rabbit pulled out of a hat. The prestige is what stuns people and it's what rounds out the act. It completes the whole spectacle.

The resurrection was Jesus' prestige. Without it only part of the story is complete. If matters were left with Jesus on the cross then it's not the whole story. He had to be brought back.

You see, life is full of suffering. The preceding sentence is the mother of all understatements for some people. It's hard and it's sometimes full of misery, pain and awfulness. Simply put, in the Christian faith the cross echoes all of this. Jesus final hours are a testimony to life being hard. But if that was where the story ended, if Jesus was left on the cross then our entire faith would be left without a sliver of hope.

No one had come back before, by themselves. No one else had shown that death could be conquered. And truthfully without the resurrection we'd still be unsure.

Jesus' resurrection is the jet-blast of hope that punches through the clouds. It's the light that shows us that there is hope, that there is life after death and that all of this pain, all of this suffering and all of this despair isn't the end.

If Jesus was left on the cross then our faith would be one to be pitied above all else. We wouldn't know for sure that death wasn't the end. But now we know for good.

So is it easy to believe in the resurrection? Is it straightforward? As with everything else in Jesus life, no! Rather annoyingly for some He doesn't perform more spectacle. He doesn't wow the crowds. He doesn't appear to the masses (not at first, anyways), and He doesn't arrive back with another star, another 3 wise men or with any sort of fanfare at all.

This wasn't the old way though, remember. He wasn't being resurrected with a pillar of fire or a pillar of smoke. If He had then chances are the people would have done exactly the same as in the Old testament and ultimately exactly what Matt wrote them as doing; they'd have been impressed at first and then would have fallen away. Why? Because to believe takes effort and we humans seem to cling to things that require a little bit of personal input. If something is thrust on our plate we get complacent. And so here's where faith kicks in.

Why does "playing hard to get" work?! Because people need a bit of chase in their love lives to keep them going. Anyone who's every had a desperate, pawing partner can attest to the fact that it makes you complacent and that it can put you off them even. Faith, I believe, is somewhat explained by God playing hard to get.

Could He have announced the resurrection with an angelic fanfare? Sure.

Could He have made Jesus turn up at Pilate's door, to prove Him wrong? Certainly.

Could He have, in fact, forced every single member of the baying crowd to believe? Definitely.

But, as I keep saying, the old way was gone. God wanted us – in part - to start chasing Him. In Christ's death and resurrection He paved the way to allowing anyone to believe and anyone to be saved. But it would take faith. It would take a bit of chasing. It would take personal effort. God would, through His grace, grant us the faith to believe, sure. But we would still take part in the chase.

Bizarrely, it works. It's that effort that spurs us on. Anything we commit ourselves to becomes more than just a chore, it becomes a passion. Anything that takes time and effort and sometimes personal sacrifice becomes a <u>big deal</u> in our lives. Faith is essential in making us believe more and more as we search deeper and deeper. If God had handed it to us on a plate, if there was DVD footage of Jesus rolling the stone away with His bare hands then chances are we'd have put the DVD away long ago and moved on.

From a Christian perspective, how many of us have been to a big mission event, have got so pumped up in worship and fervor, have made so many promises and bold pledges only to have those get broken when real life carries on? Don't get me wrong, there is nothing wrong with big mission events but my point is simple; God is as much about faith in the quiet times as he is in the spectacle. He is as much about us believing in Him when He <u>doesn't</u> do anything as He is when He does.

In the resurrection God really gets rid of a lot of the tangible stuff that we can wrap our minds around and introduces a little concept called 'faith' into humanity.

The resurrection was the completion of a mission that seemingly did everything it could to be the exact reversal of what was expected of it from the Jewish Old Testament experience;

Instead of starting out in Eden, Jesus begins His ministry in the wilderness in an anything but perfect scenario.

Instead of pillars of smoke and fire He sits on the shores of the sea and chats with regular folks.

Instead of food from Heaven He multiplies fish and bread, sits down and has long meals with friends.

Instead of destroying entire cities to prove that He is Lord He says to love your enemy and turn the other cheek.

Instead of using big-time judges, kings, priests and people of influence He uses a bunch of fishermen, tax collectors; simple, uneducated folks that changed the world.

Instead of performing miraculous signs and wonders on a regular basis He says things like, "Why does this generation ask for a miraculous sign? I tell you the truth; no sign will be given to it." (Mark 8:12).

Instead of rising up in power and showing that He is God He lets Himself be hung on a cross for the sins of mankind.

And instead of coming back with fire from heaven He appears in a garden to a few women.

(As a side note it's fascinating to see how the resurrection actually occurred. Not only did it not happen in front of tons of people, not only did the disciples not really know what was

going on at first but as I said the folks that Jesus and some angels appeared to first were women (Matthew 28:1-10, Mark 16:1-10, Luke 24:1-8).

Now, this is not a sexist statement at all, but it does hold a fascinating insight into Gods desire. During that day and age a woman's word held very little credibility at all. There were some rabbis and religious folk who would not even allow a woman to be a witness in a court of law because, to them their word held no value or authority.

And yet who does Jesus appear to first? Who does He require to go and convince the disciples? Who does He rely on as witnesses for the rest of humanity?!

From the very first moment that Jesus' resurrection was made known to mankind (and womankind) our faith in God's power over mankind's self-imposed-righteousness was being put to the test!)

Now despite these changes in tactic God hadn't changed a bit in Himself over the centuries. It was His way of reaching mankind that had. The resurrection was the final piece of the jigsaw. It showed us tangibly that He had power over death but also showed us quietly that faith was now about more than presenting your sacrifice to the priest. Faith became personal, belief became intrinsic and God became more than just a cultural identity. Before the resurrection this faith was in something external alone. Now faith moved internally as well.

When Jesus said to His disciples "come and follow me" it was an act of faith for them to leave their livelihood and go off to begin their ministry. (Mark 1:17). He didn't precede it with fireballs or seal it with parting the river Jordan. He just said it, knowing it would take faith to accomplish. Their personal belief in Him was as important as their external viewing of the miracles he performed.

Even when He did do the miraculous, when Jesus had Peter come out to Him on the water it was a personal act of faith that kept him afloat. Peter had to believe despite everything physically and emotionally telling him he would sink. (Matthew 14:22-31).

When the Centurion's servant was sick and he knew that Jesus was the only one who could help it was an act of personal faith that allowed Jesus to be able to help this man. Yes, he'd probably seen miracles happen to others but he had no reason to believe it would happen to him, a Roman. He believed, he asked, he had faith and it worked. (Matthew 8:5-10).

When the woman who had been subject to bleeding for 12 years needed healing it was by her faith in Jesus that He made it happen. She didn't earn it, deserve it or ask for it even and yet her faith allowed her to be healed (Luke 8:43-48).

Finally (and this is crucial) when Jesus explained to them what had to happen to Him, that the son of man would be betrayed, it required a great amount of faith to trust and believe Him. Even though Jesus said He would return, after His death it took maybe the biggest leap of faith yet for them to believe. What is fascinating is that again, just like the Israelites thousands of years before them, despite having seen Gods physical works close up for 3 years the disciples still fell away. They still struggled to believe - until Jesus came back. The prestige sealed their amazement and kick started the early church. This is why the resurrection is the root of our faith.

From the time He rose again the issue was and has been about faith. So did the resurrection actually help us with our faith?

Well even after seeing with their own eyes, even after He did reveal himself to them some still didn't believe. I am always fascinated by the various stories of the disciples and those closest to Jesus who still struggled to believe. I mean they watched Him die on a cross and then get buried in a tomb, sealed by a giant boulder and now here He was, walking around, talking, teleporting ("though the doors were locked, Jesus came and stood among them...") eating some fish and showing His wounds. How on earth could you struggle to believe at this point?!

I guess part of me might understand the struggle if all they did was hear rumors of this resurrection or if all they heard was the word on the street that Jesus was alive and hanging out at people's houses, but how is it possible not to believe if they actually saw the physical resurrected body of Jesus?!

Jesus isn't even coy. He relents at one point to prove His real existence. In John 20:24-29, we see what happened with good ol' "doubting Thomas".

Jesus had just appeared to all the other disciples and they had told Thomas about it. These were guys closer to Thomas than anyone and yet he still wasn't buying it. If my best friend in the world told me anything under the sun, and he believed it with all his heart then I like to think that I would believe it as well, so it's hard to understand Thomas' hesitation.

Even if I can maybe look past his refusal to believe from reliable witnesses, I don't know how I'd get past this next part. All the disciples are hanging out in a locked room that nobody should be able to get in to and then all of a sudden Jesus comes and stands among them. Just the fact that someone was able to "poof" into the room would have sold me, but then add to the fact that it was the miracle worker <u>Jesus</u> would probably have sealed the deal.

But, it didn't. Thomas still had to see and feel the wounds on Jesus' body in order for him to stop doubting and believe. Only then did he have faith.

It's interesting at this point to wonder why the gospel writers included the story of Thomas. You'd think that they'd only include stories of people believing, to give credibility to their own faith. So why was Thomas' tale written down? It could be argued, perhaps, that this act was itself added as a statement of reliability for the future believers. Even the most skeptical, the most fervent disbelievers could surely now be won-over from this testimony of a fellow doubter, right?

But the gospels don't just stop with Thomas. In Matthew 28:16-17, it says "Then the eleven disciples went to Galilee, to the mountain where Jesus had told them to go. When they saw him, they worshiped him; but some doubted."

Let's just read that again; when they saw Him they worshiped Him, but some doubted?!

Let me rephrase the emphasis; When they saw Him, some of them doubted?!

Some of the Eleven? Some of the guys who were the absolute closest to Him still doubted even when they actually set their own eyes upon Him?!

Are you kidding me?! Why aren't these people, who are physically seeing Jesus now the most ardent believers? Why do some still doubt? And worst of all – why are the gospel writers seemingly taking away the validity of the resurrection by telling me that people didn't believe?!!

I think it's clear why, actually. Jesus later makes a very significant statement that relates to those who did believe in Him;

He says in John 20:29, "...Because you have seen me, you believed; blessed are those who have not seen and yet have believed."

The gospel writers tell us about doubters because we all will face a choice about the resurrection. To doubt, or to believe. Nothing is forced on us; it is about a choice we each make. Some had personal faith, some didn't. We can all relate to one side or the other.

Hebrews 11:1 says, "Now faith is being sure of what we hope for and certain of what we do not see."

I believe that they include these tales of doubt because, for some people, even seeing won't be enough. Some people will hear about Jesus their whole lives and still not believe. Some people in Israel saw oceans swept aside like curtains and still chose the golden calf. Some people saw city walls crumble before their very eyes and chose other gods. And some people saw Jesus raised from the dead and still doubted.

This happens because these people are just like me. Full of sin and in need of a savior. Faith isn't something pressed onto us, it's something we cultivate with Christ's help or let die. God gives us the grace and faith to believe but we are involved with keeping it watered.

And so the resurrection really did turn a corner in mankind's religious life. No longer was it about what we do, where we go to church, how many verses we have memorized, how impressive our buildings are, how good the band is, how many people we witnessed to last week, how many converts we've chalked up, how well behaved we are, or any of the other things that so many folks were caught up with in Jesus' day and still seem to get caught up in now.

Plain and simple, it now became about our faith. Let me show you what the bible goes on to say after the resurrection;

"This righteousness from God comes through faith in Jesus Christ to all who believe."
(Romans 3:22)

"Therefore, since we have been justified through faith, we have peace with God through our Lord Jesus Christ, through whom we have gained access by faith into this grace in which we now stand."
(Romans 5:1-2)

"...know that a man is not justified by observing the law, but by faith in Jesus Christ. So we, too, have put our faith in Christ Jesus that we may be justified by faith in Christ and not by observing the law, because by observing the law no one will be justified."
(Galatians 2:16)

"But the Scripture declares that the whole world is a prisoner of sin, so that what was promised, being given through faith in Jesus Christ, might be given to those who believe."
(Galatians 3:22)

"You are all sons of God through faith in Christ Jesus."
(Galatians 3:26)

"But whatever was to my profit I now consider loss for the sake of Christ. What is more, I consider everything a loss compared to the surpassing greatness of knowing Christ Jesus my Lord, for whose sake I have lost all things. I consider them rubbish, that I may gain Christ and be found in him, not having a righteousness of my own that comes from the law, but that which is through faith in Christ— the righteousness that comes from God and is by faith."
(Philippians 3:7-9)

"And without faith it is impossible to please God."
(Hebrews 11:6)

The resurrection truly turned a corner indeed.

Faith is at the center of the Christian story and it all revolves around the resurrection. It is by this faith that we are truly saved;

"...if you confess with your mouth, 'Jesus is Lord', and <u>believe in your heart</u> that God raised Him from the dead, you will be saved"
(Romans 10 v 9)

Faith in the resurrection, faith in the final prestige is what seals our hope in God. No longer is God a God of pillars of smoke or pillars of fire. No longer can we simply rely on what we see of His

179

actions we're called to believe based on His one final action, the resurrection.

Because of the resurrection we can have faith in Him despite the fact that some things just don't make sense.

Because of His resurrection we can have faith even when the road map hasn't been laid out before us.

We can have faith no matter what the world might throw at us because we know the outcome of our story through the knowledge of the resurrection.

The resurrection is a perfect ending to the "old way of doing things" not because it ties everything up nice and sweet and answers all our questions, but because it sets up the way that God wants to function in humanity. Not as a genie in a bottle, appearing every now and again to part seas or wipe out enemies, but as a God that lives in each of us and functions through faith. A God that wants to be chased, as much as He chases. A God that desires love, as much as obedience. Like any other father on the planet God wants more than anything for His children to just be madly in love with Him and He wants us to choose to want to be with Him.

And so the resurrection is a huge challenge to each of us;

It challenges our intellectual side: can we really believe that a human being died, that blood stopped flowing through His veins, that His heart stopped pumping, that breath no longer flowed in and out of His lungs and then, 3 days later, He pops up and starts living life again? Can we have faith, despite the fact that this seemingly doesn't make biological sense?

It challenges our religious side; can we really let go of the way we have done things for thousands of years? Can we really let go of this system of works and religious achievements that always kept us in check? Can we really allow for the fact that anyone, regardless of how "bad" they might be can simply have faith in Jesus Christ, and find salvation in Him?

It challenges our emotional side; Can I have faith in my Savior, no matter the circumstance? Can I still have faith when I lose a family member? Can I still have faith when life is hard? Can I still have faith when life is as far from where I'd want it to be as possible? Can I still have faith in this Savior of mine when it seems like I got the raw end of the deal or when He is silent?

And it challenges our spiritual side; can my heart have faith in something I cannot see, smell or touch? Can my heart believe in something that seems too good to be true? Can I genuinely have faith and be sure of what I hope for and certain of what I cannot see? Can my faith overcome my humanity?

Every one of these is a step of faith and this is exactly what the resurrection challenges us with. This is why the resurrection is the beginning of "the new way of doing things."

Lastly then, to finish off I just want to look at what Jesus actually does in the short time that He did return. Even when He came back part of me would have wanted to see Jesus spend a good year or so reaffirming all that He had taught them. He could've definitely used the greatest "I told you so" event in history to back up all His teachings.

It just seems natural that after such an incredible comeback He would spend some quality time making sure all His followers really did know exactly what to preach, what to emphasize and how to convey it accurately.

So why did He cut His time after the resurrection so short?

I think it again stems from faith. But this is not just a one-sided affair.

It is not just about our faith in Jesus.

It is also about <u>His</u> faith in us.

For some unknown reason Jesus had faith that these fishermen could get the job done. Don't forget that when He returned they'd abandoned Him, gone back to fishing, disobeyed Him, lied about Him, forgotten all He'd told them and had stopped practicing what He'd instructed them! Why on earth would He suddenly trust them again?!

For some reason He cut His time short because He believed that these guys (along with the power of the Holy Spirit, given in Pentecost) could go on and impact the world. He effectively left them with the greatest pat-on-the-back in history and said;

"All authority in Heaven and on earth has been given to me. Therefore go and make disciples of all nations, baptizing them in the name of the Father and of the Son and of the Holy Spirit."

God showed that He had faith in them.

Previously God had been the one leading. All the events of the Old testament point to a God leading ahead of His people. Parting the sea to let them across. Knocking down walls to gain them entry. Wiping out armies to let them vanquish.

Now suddenly God has moved places. Now He's behind them, pushing them forwards.

Let's use an analogy that's close to home. Matt's just had a little boy, Noah. He's only 3 months old at the moment and Matt is very much in charge of that little boy's life. He's leading the way, he's showing him what to do, how to eat, how to live and what not to do. As he grows up sometimes Matt is going to have to be hard on him, to smack his hands to stop him hurting himself, to say "no" and listen to him screaming in retaliation.

But one thing is clear. That cannot last forever. Matt cannot do that for Noah when he's 21! At some point Matt is going to shift position and go from leading Noah on to pushing him forwards.

Noah is going to have to start living, to start trying to work out how to be a man. Everything Matt does in the early days will act as preparation and foundation for his life but at some point Noah will have to find his own feet.

The resurrection is a similar turning point for us. God now says "I believe in you". "You go and make fishers of men". "You feed my sheep".

The emphasis, after the resurrection, slips from being all about worshipping God in a temple on a set day, about following every letter of His law, about trailing behind Him in obedience and becomes about us each stepping forward with His Holy Spirit in our heart.

It becomes about us taking our first steps as Christians with God inside us and pushing us forwards rather than dragging us onwards.

Will God prompt us, guide us, inspire us and point us in the right direction? Yes, very much so. Is He still the same almighty God, worthy of fear, worthy of honor, worthy of ultimate respect and obedience? Certainly.

But now it's up to us to play our part. The resurrection shifts the emphasis from God, to us. After He has been raised for a short while humanity no longer has the physical embodiment of God with us; Jesus ascends to heaven. He's gone physically and we're left on our own. Now we're called to strive ahead with His Spirit inside us, His example in front of us and all His power and might behind us.

Jesus only stayed a short while because that's all He needed to do. Ultimately if you doubt whether the resurrection took place as it should have, look at what happens afterwards; it works. The church explodes, people believe without seeing, miracles happen from previous-sinners like Peter and Paul and history shows that...it worked!

We're here today because it worked. I'm writing this today because the resurrection worked! No, it didn't happen as Matt would have done it or as I would have done it but I think the end of Matt's version is pretty poignant – however we would have done it probably would have failed. The way Jesus did it actually worked.

I am here today as a testament to the fact that the resurrection of Jesus Christ, changes lives. I am going to heaven because of what He did on the cross and because I believe that He was raised from the dead. I cannot write anything more clearer than this - I am a sinner, saved by God through Jesus Christ, the way He did it! So is Matt. So are all who have faith in the Jesus who died and is risen.

Epilogue

The truth is simple; I am so unbelievably glad that I'm not Jesus.

I am so unbelievably grateful that God did it His way and not the way I would have done it. There are many times when I'd like to be God and certainly Anna, my wife will tell you that there are many times when I act like I think I am. But the truth is simple – God knows what He's doing and I don't have a clue.

No, Jesus' ways don't always make sense to me. I don't understand why He plays hard to get sometimes. I don't understand why He doesn't wipe the floor with satan, why in the gospels He doesn't come back and individually knock on the Pharisees doors to deliver a Messianic roundhouse kick to the face for each and every of them. I certainly would have, if I was Him.

But I guess this is the point. I'm in the story; I'm not the author of it. God writes Himself into our storyline as Christ and ultimately He's in charge of how it's written, not me. If I was in charge it would end in disaster. It's been so easy over the past year as my little boy's been ill to genuinely believe that I know better than God. That I know how my story should play out and what God should be doing for me. That He isn't in charge and that if I was I'd do a better job of it.

But the truth of the matter is that as a character in this story of life I don't have editing rights. I don't know what's coming around the corner and as such I don't know how the story should play out. Too often have I tried to "play God" and assume that if I was Him I would do a better job all round. But really I know what would happen.

In the time that it's taken me to write this book my wife has had a baby, I've been promoted at work, one of our dogs has bitten me by accident and I finally got around to fully knocking down that shed. My life's story is carrying on as normal - exceedingly normally-so - except for me having an incredible son and an amazingly undeserved wife.

I have all the normal concerns of men my age; can I pay the bills, am I keeping fit, how am I doing at work, why cant I fix my mountain bike, and how do I stop getting grey nasal hair?

Nearing 32 it is odd to think that Jesus was a guy physically like myself. I often wonder what His concerns were. What went through His mind when he lay in bed? I often wonder about what He thought about, sitting by the campfire in the evenings with the disciples, glancing over at Judas night after night. When He looked at His other friends, knowing full well that they'd desert Him, what did He think about their bold and brash claims to always follow Him?

When he spoke to crowds and could read the thoughts behind their faces, what did it make Him want to do? How did He cope with having Pharisees around? How could He look the people who would kill Him in the eye and show love to them, daily?

In a years' time hopefully we'll have moved house down to Reading, where my wife comes from. Noah will be nearing 3 and perhaps we'll have another baby by then too. Maybe I'll be a Station Commander by that point and perhaps I'll have finally gotten around to growing the moustache that I keep threatening Anna I'll one day sport.

At 33, Jesus was dead. At 30 He knew this. Each and every day He had to speak to people, heal people and love people, many of whom He knew would be in the crowd baying for His blood. He had to perform miracles knowing people wouldn't believe in them. He had to impart heavenly wisdom knowing that people were more interested in the free fish.

At 33 He had to talk Himself into getting crucified, knowing that at any minute He could get Himself out of it. He had to allow the very bags of skin and bones that He'd created, that He'd watched grow up, that He'd loved and cared for strap Him to a tree and drive nails into Him.

He had to hang there knowing that 2000-odd years later a man called Matt Chapman would screw up being a Christian, mess up daily and still claim to love Him. And yet He still went ahead and died for me.

I am so unbelievably glad that I'm not Jesus.

I hope you've got something out of this book, even if it's simply that Jesus' way worked. JR, I thank you for bringing the wisdom, the credentials and the general air of sensibleness to all of this.

As for me, I'm off to hide before I'm given more garden work to do.

Thanks for reading.

The End.

www.ingramcontent.com/pod-product-compliance
Lightning Source LLC
Chambersburg PA
CBHW060241050426
42448CB00009B/1549